A Little Guide

GROW
YOUR
FAITH

CHUCK ALLEN &
BOBBY MCGRAW

Grow Your Faith: A Little Guide to Bigger Faith

Copyright © 2024 by Chuck Allen and Bobby McGraw

First Edition: September 2024

ISBN: 9798336109542

Cover and Interior design by Steve Plummer, SPBookDesign.com

Printed in the United States of America

TABLE OF CONTENTS

INTRODUCTION

H I FRIEND. THIS book is written for you and is an invitation to grow spiritually. We firmly believe that you can grow, and in fact, you were created to grow.

We wrote this book because we often encounter people who feel stuck, some deeply stuck in their spiritual journeys. It's not uncommon to feel stuck. It can be an overwhelming and frustrating experience. We certainly don't want you to stay there.

How do you know if you are stuck? Here are a few of the top symptoms we've seen and experienced:

- **Frustration and Discontent:** It's not uncommon to feel frustrated when we don't see progress in our spiritual journey. It can leave us feeling deeply discontented, wondering why our efforts aren't bearing fruit.

- **Confusion and Doubt:** It's common to experience confusion about our faith. We start questioning our beliefs and, at times, doubting our relationship with God. This can make us feel less stable and provokes uncertainty.

- **Apathy and Lack of Motivation:** When it seems like we're stuck and not moving forward, it's easy to become apathetic. We lose motivation to engage in spiritual practices because they start to feel meaningless or ineffective.

If you've felt any of these symptoms (or more), congratulations, you're normal! But like we said, we don't want you to stay there. By recognizing these feelings, we can begin to address them and seek God's guidance to move forward in our spiritual growth.

HOW TO GET THE MOST OUT OF THIS BOOK:

This book is a guided journey toward spiritual growth, written by two friends and pastors who are committed to this lifelong journey. We don't claim to have "arrived," but we are dedicated to growing every day. We both believe that all of us, no matter our backgrounds, can know God and spend the rest of our lives growing to become more and more like Jesus.

As pastors, we are primarily practitioners, and this book is meant to be exceedingly practical. While there certainly is a place in our libraries for theological treatises, we have written this book for you, a normal person who desires to grow while also working, raising your children, studying, and everything else that is common practice in our lives today.

Your Invitation to Grow is divided into several entries or chapters. While you might choose to read straight through, we encourage you to take your time with each entry, allowing time to reflect and apply the truths you encounter. Some entries are designed to share a truth we've learned, and others are intended to spark action. Certain themes will be revisited along the way to reinforce your growth. These themes hit differently depending on where you are in your journey.

No matter the style of each entry, our prayer is that you will be equipped and inspired to take your next step in spiritual growth.

We reference or quote a lot of scripture in this book. When doing so, we've used several Bible translations that we've found helpful, including the New Living Translation, the English Standard Version, the New American Standard Bible, and the New International Version.

Welcome to your spiritual growth path. Enjoy the journey!

CHUCK ALLEN & BOBBY MCGRAW
FALL 2024

CHAPTER 1

GET OUT OF THE BOAT TO GROW

J UMPING INTO THE unknown is scary. When I was 10 years old, my dad thought it was a good idea to send me to an overnight boy's club camp. I didn't know a single soul there, but Dad thought it might toughen me up. On the second day of camp, we went to the lake to swim. There was a cliff that we could jump off that was about 20 ft. high. From the top, through the eyes of a 10-year-old, it looked like the cliffs I saw on Wide World of Sports. It looked more like 120 ft. high. When it was time to take the plunge, I stood there frozen in my tracks. It was only when the rest of the boys, especially the older dudes that had been there before, started making fun of me that I finally jumped. I must have been more terrified of their picking on me than I was to jump, so away I went...feet first and no holding of the nose. I DIDN'T DIE!

IT'S TIME TO JUMP

I learned a super growth lesson that day: **Sometimes we must face our fears, embrace adventure, and take the plunge. Sometimes we simply need to jump.**

But what holds us back from risking it all? How do we overcome our fears? What do we do when we doubt the next chapter of life God is writing for us? How do we keep our eyes focused on the goal when everything is trying to distract us?

It's easy to criticize others like a Monday morning quarterback; it's something else to stand in the pocket and take the hits.

Peter breaks it down for us as he jumps, not off a cliff, but out of a boat. In Matthew 14, we read about Peter walking on the water, and if we look closely enough, we may just discover the courage to follow his example.

You really must love how these verses reveal more of Peter's character. He reminds me of myself because he is quick to act, often without thinking. Peter is a ready-fire-aim kind of guy. He shoots off his mouth when shutting up may be the better choice.

Peter understood failure. After all, he denied Jesus three times. But he also experienced the grace of forgiveness, and he had the joy of God using him mightily on the day of Pentecost. Peter also preached the sermon that led about 5,000 people to put their faith in Jesus.

Peter gets a bad rap for walking on the water and then losing faith and sinking. I don't think that's necessarily fair.

Jesus does call Peter a man of little faith, but what about the other eleven disciples? None of them got out of the boat. If Peter had little faith, then they had none. It's easy to criticize others like a Monday morning quarterback; it's something else to stand in the pocket and take the hits.

WHAT KEEPS US IN THE BOAT?

When it comes to trusting Jesus, what keeps us from getting out of the boat? What keeps you from daring to trust Jesus? Let's look at the reasons we are afraid to leave the boat, and the way Peter overcame them. I want us to dare to trust Jesus completely.

DARING TO TRUST JESUS COMPLETELY

1. Discourage Disillusionment

Our fears can disillusion us and distort our thoughts.

When the disciples first see Jesus coming at them they mistake Him for a ghost. They spent the whole night afraid the storm would drown them, and now a ghost shows up. Things were going from bad to worse.

The first thing that must happen to get out of the boat is that our disillusionment must be discouraged.

Have you ever noticed that we make the problems of life worse in our head than they really are? We often make our fears greater than they are. But how do we manage real fears?

We must know the person of Jesus.

Do you know how they train federal agents to spot counterfeit money? They put them in a room for days and have them count real money. Then, after days of counting real money, they slip a phony bill in. More often than not, the agent will catch the fake dollar. Why? Not because they know everything there is about counterfeit money, but because they are so familiar with the original that anything apart from the original is obvious. That's how we must become.

We must become so familiar with Jesus, that when false promises show up, we spot them for who they are and where they come from. We must know Jesus in the deepest most personal sense. Only when Peter is sure that it is Jesus walking on the water does he dare think about getting out of the boat.

How is your relationship with Jesus? Is His voice louder than the voice of fear in your head?

2. Defeat Distractions

Distractions often keep us from seeing Jesus in the midst of the storm.

Peter leaves the boat when he knows that it is Jesus on the water and not a ghost, and for a little while he walks on the water. Peter does the impossible, but then things change. Peter took his eyes off Jesus and focused on the storm. When Peter got out of the boat, he focused on Jesus—on the source of his power. Then, Peter shifted his focus from the source of his power to the problems that surrounded him, and he started to sink.

We will sink when we get distracted from Jesus, our source of power. Distractions can come in two forms: the **obvious** and the **subtle**. We get scared by things that look like they will overtake us, and we turn from Jesus, the source of our power and peace. When we choose to focus on the problems rather than the power, we sacrifice our connection with Jesus.

Jesus is a power greater than the problems we face. When our problems distract us from Jesus, we turn from the greatest power there is to a lesser power. John writes in 1 John 4:4 "...the one who is in you is greater than the one who is in the world." If we focus on the problems then we will lose sight of the One greater than anything.

3. Destroy Doubt

Undealt with doubt can be very dangerous. When Peter got into the boat, the disciples worshiped Jesus. We get the feeling that this worship of Him was different. Amazingly, this is not a first-time event for the disciples. Earlier, in Matthew chapter 8, the disciples are in the boat when a storm comes up. The storm is so bad that they think they will die. Sound familiar? Only instead of walking on water, Jesus is asleep in the boat. The disciples wake Jesus, and He speaks to the wind and the waves and the storm calms. The disciples look at one another and say, "What kind of man is this? - even the winds and the sea obey him!" (Matthew 8:27). Compare this with what they confess in chapter 14:33, when they say that Jesus is the Son of God. How did they get from, "What kind of man is this?" to "You are the Son of God" (Matthew 14:33)?

Something about the whole experience opened their eyes to the power and ability of Jesus. Before this encounter, Jesus was just an amazing man, but now the disciples saw Him as the Messiah and Son of God. So, how can we see

Jesus for who He really is? How can we move from seeing Jesus as just a great man, to the only One who can change our lives?

We must spend time with Him. It is simple, but sometimes it is the most obvious thing that we fail to see. To know Jesus, we must spend time with Jesus. When the storms of life come, how long will you wait 'till you call on Jesus? We often try to think our way out of problems and search for others who can get us out of them before we look to Jesus. Why is Jesus not our first refuge in difficult times? Not only must Jesus be our first choice, but He must also become our only choice. Following Jesus is a leap of faith, like jumping off the cliff. We can't play it safe and follow Jesus. We must be willing to risk it all. Could it be that you have allowed fears to become greater than they really are? Are problems distracting you from the source of your power? Do doubts nag at you and keep you from running to Jesus?

Whatever it is, Jesus is greater than your fears, problems, and doubts. Jesus is waiting on you to believe in Him and risk it all. Come on, leave the boat and walk on the water. Jesus says you can do it.

Growth often starts with a leap
into the unknown. It's in those scary
moments that God stretches our faith
and builds our courage. Take the jump!

*"So be strong and courageous, all you
who put your hope in the Lord!"*
— PSALM 31:24

16

CHAPTER 2

SURRENDERING: WHITE FLAG OR CHECKERED FLAG?

HAVE YOU EVER had one of those days where you just wanted to wave the white flag and give up? I know I have. In fact, just this past Tuesday, I found myself in that exact place. I told my wife Jen that I just wanted to quit. I was done.

It's a hard thing to admit as a pastor. I mean, I've got one of the greatest gigs on the planet, right? But the truth is, we all have those moments where life feels overwhelming, and we want to surrender to our circumstances.

Growing up in Daytona Beach, Florida, I was surrounded by racing culture. In racing, the white flag means there's one lap left, which sounds like a good thing if you're in the lead. But in warfare, waving a white flag means something very different. It's a sign of defeat, of giving up.

I'm afraid many of us treat life like we want to wave that white flag of defeat. We look at our circumstances— the anxiety, the bad diagnoses, the wayward children, the financial struggles—and we feel like giving up. We want to surrender to our problems rather than to God.

But what if surrender didn't have to mean defeat? What if, instead of waving a white flag, we could wave a checkered flag of victory?

I once heard a definition of surrender, "to cease resistance to an enemy or opponent and submit to their authority."

That sounds pretty negative, doesn't it? It conjures up images of a battered army crawling out of their trenches in defeat.

When we talk about surrendering to Jesus, it's not about waving a white flag of defeat.

But surrender doesn't always have to be negative. Sometimes, surrendering the wrong things can put us on the right track. If your business is heading in the wrong direction because of poor choices, surrendering those choices and changing course could lead to success. If your marriage is struggling, surrendering your pride and selfish attitudes could breathe new life into your relationship.

When we talk about surrendering to Jesus, it's not about waving a white flag of defeat. It's about exchanging our way for His way, and His way leads to victory.

The apostle Paul puts it this way in Colossians 3:1–4:

> *Since, then, you have been raised with Christ, set your hearts on things above, where Christ is, seated at the right hand of God. Set your minds on things above, not on earthly things. For you died, and your life is now hidden with Christ in God. When Christ, who is your life, appears, then you also will appear with him in glory.*

Paul is reminding us that when we put our faith in Christ, we die to our old way of life because we are then raised to new life in Him. Our real life is now hidden with Christ in God.

This is the beauty of the Christian faith. So many religions are built on what you have to do to earn your way to paradise. But the message of Jesus essentially says, "I've already done everything you need. All you have to do is surrender to me and you get it all."

The problem is, many of us are willing to trust Jesus for eternity but not for today. We'll trust Him for heaven, but not for our board meeting on Tuesday. We'll trust Him with our eternal soul, but not with our finances, or our health, or our relationships.

But Jesus didn't come just to keep us out of hell. He came to walk with us through every mess of life. He wants us to experience His peace, His joy, His grace right now— not just in the sweet by and by.

Our willingness to surrender to God's will comes from believing that what we gain in Jesus is worth far more than any cost associated with serving Him. When we choose to pursue Jesus—which is the very will of God—we surrender:

- The ambitions we could never achieve on our own
- The control we never really had over our lives anyway
- The comfort that was never in our power to maintain
- The life we could never sustain or orchestrate ourselves

- In exchange, we gain the abundant life Jesus promised—a life of purpose, peace, and joy that can't be shaken by circumstances.

But to fully surrender and experience God's best for us, we've got to give up our determination to control our own lives. Our Creator made us to need Him, He wired us to want to worship Him, and He designed us to be in desperate relationship with Him. Yet, God is not a puppet master pulling our strings. He wants us to choose Him, to say, "I trust you. I surrender. Let's do this."

It's like every morning when you wake up, God (who never slumbers) is standing there by your bed. As you rub the sleep from your eyes and stumble to the coffee pot, He says, "Alright, we're gonna play in my sandbox all day. Let's go racing!"

Some of us respond, "Nah, I'm just gonna wait for heaven. I'm good." And then we go through our day wondering why our life seems so out of sorts.

So, what does practical surrender look like? Let me give you three tangible examples:

1. **Commit to spending just 5 minutes each morning in God's Word.** Download a Bible app, pick a 5-day reading plan, and get Scripture into your life. Even if you don't memorize it, God's Word will go to work in your heart all day long.

2. **Pray a simple prayer each day.** It doesn't have to be long or fancy. Pray something as simple as,

"God, today would you give me wisdom? Would you grant me greater peace? Would you help me build better relationships?" That takes less than 20 seconds, but it invites God into your day.

3. **Follow Jesus' example in baptism.** Jesus was baptized as an example for us, and He commanded us to be baptized as well. Yet, so many of us let our pride keep us from this simple act of obedience and identification with Christ.

These may seem like small steps, but they represent a heart that is surrendered to God's will rather than our own. They show we're willing to trust Him not just with eternity, but with our daily lives.

The truth is, when we try to take total control of our lives, we're attempting to do what only God can handle. The struggle between our knowledge of God's character and our conflicting emotions is an ongoing battle. It will never be fully over until we get to heaven.

But if we can trust a God who knew us before we were formed in our mother's womb, who knows every hair on our head and every thought before we think it, surely we can trust Him with our daily lives.

As Jeremiah 29:11 reminds us, "'For I know the plans I have for you,' says the Lord. 'They are plans for good and not for disaster, to give you a future and a hope.'"

When our view of God becomes small and our problems loom large, that's when we need to surrender afresh. We need to bring Him all our junk and take on all His joy. We can trust our hearts in His hands.

As we've read before, Proverbs 3:5–6 puts it this way, "Trust in the Lord with all your heart; do not depend on your own understanding. Seek his will in all you do, and he will show you which path to take."

He is trustworthy when we doubt, forgiving when we fail, selfless when we are selfish, and tender when we're broken.

In other words, the decision is already made—we just need to follow where He leads. But how do we know it's God leading? If you spend time with God, you'll know His voice. If you don't spend time with Him, you'll always be questioning. God didn't make this complicated, we did. He is trustworthy when we doubt, forgiving when we fail, selfless when we are selfish, and tender when we're broken. His unconditional love soothes us. When we surrender, we get it all.

Maybe we just don't really believe Romans 8:28: "And we know that God causes everything to work together for the good of those who love God and are called according to his purpose for them."

If that's the case, then my entire life is a joke. Except for this one thing: in the worst moments of my life, He was there. I knew it, I felt it, and I still feel it and know it today. You see, when we surrender, we get all that He offers, plus we get Him. He is good when the sun shines on our joy-filled life, and He is good when our life is falling apart. God is always good.

So, the question is: why don't you surrender today?

Settle your heart and surrender yourself to Christ. It starts with recognizing that you're not perfect and that your bad choices and sin have separated you from God. But God sent Jesus to pay the price for your imperfection and sin. Jesus died for you and rose from the dead for you. All you have to do is trust Him with your life.

Maybe you've already made that decision, but you've been waddling in spiritual mediocrity. Maybe it's time to take the next step of obedience in baptism. Or maybe you've been a Christian for years, but you need a fresh wind of God's Spirit in your life.

Whatever your situation, I challenge you to surrender afresh today. Stop waving the white flag of defeat to your circumstances and start waving the checkered flag of victory in Christ.

Surrender isn't about giving up, it's about giving over: giving over our wills, our plans, our lives to the One who loves us more than we can imagine. It's about trusting that His ways are higher than our ways, His thoughts higher than our thoughts.

When we fully surrender to Christ, we exchange our weakness for His strength, our fear for His peace, our uncertainty for His guidance. We trade our white flag of defeat for His banner of love over us.

So today, will you surrender? Will you trust Him not just with eternity, but with this day? Will you invite Him into your joys and your struggles, your victories, and your messes?

Remember, Jesus didn't come just to be your ticket to heaven. He came to be your life—your everything. He wants to walk with you through every high and every low.

He wants to transform you from the inside out, making you more like Him day by day.

Surrender isn't a one-time event. It's a daily choice, a moment-by-moment decision to trust God rather than ourselves. It's saying, "Not my will, but Yours be done" in the big decisions and the small ones.

As you go about your day, look for opportunities to surrender your will to His. When you're tempted to worry, surrender your anxiety to His peace. When you're faced with a difficult decision, surrender your wisdom for His guidance. When you're hurt or disappointed, surrender your pain to His healing touch.

Remember, in God's kingdom, surrender doesn't lead to defeat, it leads to victory. It's not about waving a white flag; it's about waving a checkered flag. So, let's go racing with Jesus today, surrendering our lives to Him and experiencing the fullness of the life He promises.

May we all have the courage to stand up and say, "Jesus, I'm all in. I surrender my life to You, not just for eternity, but for this day. Have Your way in me. Amen."

Surrender isn't waving the white flag of defeat; it's crossing the finish line in victory by trusting God with the outcome.

"The Lord will fight for you; you need only to be still."
—Exodus 14:14

CHAPTER 3

THE BIBLE IS A BIG DEAL

N THE CHRISTIAN faith, the Bible holds a place of utmost importance. That's why we quote from it so much throughout this book. It is foundational for our journey towards growth.

At our church, the phrase, "We believe the Bible is a Big Deal" is often used to emphasize the significance of this sacred text. The Bible is revered as a gift from God, a divine revelation that provides direction, correction, and inspiration to those who seek its wisdom. It is a living, breathing collection of 66 books, divinely inspired through the hearts and pens of men, serving as a life manual and a comprehensive guide to navigating the complexities of human existence.

The Word of God encompasses all of God's spoken revelation, including the teachings and life of His Son, Jesus Christ. These revelations are recorded in written form in the Scriptures, and by reading, hearing, and acting upon them, believers can avoid the confusion that often stems from cultural religion. The power of God's Word is immense, capable of exposing our deepest sins, and guiding us towards righteousness.

The author of Hebrews eloquently describes the nature of God's Word in Hebrews 4:12–13:

> *For the word of God is alive and powerful. It is sharper than the sharpest two-edged sword, cutting between soul and spirit, between joint and marrow. It exposes our innermost thoughts and desires. Nothing in all creation is hidden from God. Everything is naked and exposed before his eyes, and he is the one to whom we are accountable.*

This passage highlights three essential characteristics of the Bible: its living nature, its active power, and its ability to pierce the depths of our being.

First, God's Word is living. As God Himself is the living God, His Word cannot be separated from Him, making it a living entity. It is an indestructible force, as proclaimed in Isaiah 40:8, "The grass withers, the flower fades, but the word of our God stands forever." As the author of life, God's living Word imparts life in two distinct ways. It gives new life to those in need of Jesus, offering hope and salvation to those who seek it. Additionally, it provides renewed life to God's people of faith, revitalizing them during times of spiritual dryness when God may seem distant.

The psalmist, David, recognized the restorative power of God's Word, writing in Psalm 19:7, "The law of the Lord is perfect, restoring the soul." Throughout the 176 verses of Psalm 119, the benefits of the Bible are explored in great detail. The psalmist repeatedly cries out, "My soul cleaves to the dust; Revive me according to Your word," and "This is my comfort in my affliction, that Your word has revived me." (Psalm 119:50)

It is only logical that if the living God has spoken to us through His written Word, we should seek it like a precious treasure and consume it as a starving person devours a meal. Being the Word of God, it is both a message from God and a revelation about His nature and character.

Despite being written centuries ago, the Bible remains timeless and relevant. The Spirit of God continues to speak directly to us through its pages, addressing the very issues we face in our modern world. To fully grasp its wisdom, it is recommended to read the Bible consecutively, exploring both the Old and New Testaments. By doing so, readers often find that God uses the passages they have recently read to speak into their lives in meaningful ways.

The power of God's Word to transform lives cannot be overstated.

The power of God's Word to transform lives cannot be overstated. Even dedicating just five minutes a day to reading or listening to the Holy Scriptures can lead to radical, positive changes. These changes occur not because of the book itself, but because of the Author—the Divine Inspiration behind every word.

Second, God's Word is active. The Greek word translated as "active" is the root of our English word, "energy." It signifies that the Word is effectual, accomplishing what God intends for it to do. As Isaiah states in Isaiah 55:10–11,

For as the rain and the snow come down from heaven, and do not return there without

> *watering the earth and making it bear and sprout, and furnishing seed to the sower and bread to the eater; So will My word be which goes forth out of My mouth; It will not return to Me empty, Without accomplishing what I desire, And without succeeding in the matter for which I sent it.*

God promises that His Word will fulfill its purpose, never returning void.

Last, God's Word is sharp and piercing. Hebrews 4:12 describes it as, "...sharper than any two-edged sword, and piercing as far as the division of soul and spirit, of both joints and marrow." This figurative language illustrates that God's Word cuts deeply, reaching the very core of our being. However, God's purpose in cutting us is not to leave us wounded, but to bring healing. Just as a skilled surgeon removes a cancerous tumor, the Word of God cuts away the sin and darkness within us to bring ultimate healing and life.

In light of these truths, it is crucial to treasure God's Word above all human counsel. We must read, study, and meditate on the Scriptures, for they cannot benefit us if we remain ignorant of their contents. Moreover, we must apply, trust, and obey God's Word, allowing it to transform our hearts and lives. The purpose of studying the Bible is not merely to fill our heads with knowledge about the end times or to gather theological arguments to support our favorite views. Rather, it is to experience the life-changing power that the Word of God holds.

As we approach the Bible with a heart of obedience, we open ourselves to the incredible power it can bring to our lives. The living, active, and piercing nature of God's Word can expose our deepest sins, guide us towards righteousness, and restore our souls. It is a timeless and relevant source of wisdom, speaking directly to the challenges we face in our modern world.

So, let us embrace the Bible as the precious gift it is: a divine revelation from the living God. May we dedicate ourselves to reading, studying, and meditating on its pages, allowing the Spirit of God to speak into our lives through its timeless truths. As we apply, trust, and obey God's Word, we will experience the transformative power it holds, leading us towards a life of purpose, healing, and deep connection with our Creator.

Remember, the Bible is not just another book; it is a living, breathing testament to the love and wisdom of God. It is a big deal, and by making it a central part of our lives, we open ourselves to the incredible blessings and guidance that only the Word of God can provide.

CHAPTER 4

JESUS IS THE BIGGEST DEAL

N A WORLD that often seems to have lost sight of what truly matters, it's natural to wonder: what's the big deal with Jesus? Growing up, I remember singing songs like "Jesus, Jesus, Jesus, sweetest name I know." I've heard countless lessons and sermons emphasizing that Jesus is the answer, our hope, and that He loves us deeply. And while these messages were all true, today's climate and culture seem to have shifted. It's as if the name of Jesus has become just another name, and He has become just another way.

So, why do we make such a big deal about Jesus? Why do we boldly proclaim that the Bible is a big deal, and that Jesus is the biggest deal of all? These are valid questions that deserve thoughtful answers.

One of the most famous believers in the Bible is a man named Paul, whose story is nothing short of remarkable. For a significant portion of his life, Paul actively persecuted those who believed in Jesus. He despised Jesus and anyone who followed Him, going so far as to try to stop the emerging church by killing its early leaders.

But everything changed when Paul encountered Jesus personally. That transformative meeting altered the course of his life for the better, and he went on to write numerous letters that eventually became books of the Bible. In his letter to the Romans, Paul addresses the tension within the early church as believers sought to understand what it meant to live out the life of Christ.

In the fifth chapter of Romans, Paul opens by discussing the one thing everyone desperately needs: peace with God. And it's through these verses that we discover why Jesus is truly the biggest deal.

Why is Jesus the biggest deal? Because Jesus...

1. RESCUES US

> *For while we were still weak, at the right time Christ died for the ungodly. For one will scarcely die for a righteous person-though perhaps for a good person one would dare even to die-but God shows his love for us in that while we were still sinners, Christ died for us. (Romans 5:6-8)*

Paul explains that when we don't know Jesus, we are helpless, powerless, and cut off from God's presence. Yet, even in that state, Jesus willingly died on the cross for our sins. God sent His Son to die for the very people who refused to worship Him, revealing the immeasurable depth of His love for us.

When we find ourselves helpless, powerless, and cut off, we often think that doing the right thing will make us right with God. We reason, "Maybe if I volunteer my time,

Jesus is the Biggest Deal

give money, improve my life, or try harder to clean up my act, I can earn God's favor."

But the reality is that no matter how much we strive to do what's right, it can never make us right with God. We can't earn our way into heaven or bribe God to be on our side. Despite our best efforts, there's always a gnawing feeling inside, reminding us that our works are insufficient.

Paul clarifies that anyone who doesn't know Christ personally is at enmity with God.

At just the right time, while we were still sinners, Christ died for us. He went to the cross and redeemed us, freeing us from the burden of trying to earn our way into God's presence. We don't become Christians because we believe in our own goodness or in ourselves.

Instead, when we come to Christ, He gives us the faith and confidence to believe in Him. As we trust that His death is our own death, He liberates us from the futile endeavor of earning our way into God's presence. He rescues us from ourselves and the world.

2. RELEASES US

"For if while we were enemies we were reconciled to God by the death of his Son, much more, now that we are reconciled, shall we be saved by his life." (Romans 5:10)

Paul clarifies that anyone who doesn't know Christ personally is at enmity with God. Why? Because we are incapable of obeying God's law or fulfilling His will on our own. Condemnation means that God declares us sinners, which is essentially a declaration of war. Justification, on

35

the other hand, means that God declares us righteous, which is a declaration of peace made possible by Christ's death on the cross. Through His sacrifice, Jesus removes the hostility that existed between us and God because of our sin, making a relationship with Him possible. He releases us from our past mistakes, scars, and failures.

Jesus declares us to be something we could never attain on our own merit. Our sins are not merely covered; they are completely removed.

3. RESTORES US

"Since, therefore, we have now been justified by his blood, much more shall we be saved by him from the wrath of God." (Romans 5:9)

God hates sin because it cost Him the life of His Son. Ever since Adam and Eve's original sin, every person has been born a sinner, separated from God due to our sinful nature. Sin makes us enemies of God.

But now, because of Jesus' death, He has removed that separation and restored us to a relationship of peace with Him. Jesus paid the price for our sin, making it possible for us to experience God's presence. The reason we can now step into God's presence and know Him intimately is that Jesus made peace and restored us.

4. RECREATES US

"More than that, we also rejoice in God through our Lord Jesus Christ, through whom we have now received reconciliation." (Romans 5:11)

Eternal life is not just about going to heaven someday. Eternal life is the very life of God given to those who, by faith, know Him as their leader and allow Him to control their lives right now. When we believe in Jesus, His life is deposited within us. His presence in our lives empowers us to live the life He has called us to live.

So, why is Jesus the biggest deal?

At the end of the day, what we truly long for and desperately need is peace with God. And that peace is something we can never attain on our own. Only Jesus can provide it.

- Only Jesus can rescue us from our helpless state.

- Only Jesus can release us from the burden of our past.

- Only Jesus can restore us to a right relationship with God.

- Only Jesus can recreate us and give us new life.

- Only Jesus.

- That is a big deal. In fact, it's the biggest deal of all!

In a world that often feels chaotic, confusing, and devoid of meaning, Jesus stands as the unshakable foundation, the source of true peace, and the answer to our deepest longings. When we grasp the magnitude of what He has done for us—rescuing, releasing, restoring, and recreating us— we cannot help but make a big deal about Him.

So, let us boldly proclaim the name of Jesus, not as just another name among many, but as the name above all names.

Let us cling to the truth of His Word, the Bible, as our anchor in the storms of life. And let us invite others to experience the transformative power of knowing Jesus personally.

Because when we truly understand why Jesus is the biggest deal, our lives will never be the same. We will find ourselves filled with a peace that surpasses understanding, a joy that transcends circumstances, and a purpose that goes beyond anything this world can offer.

So, don't be afraid to make a big deal about Jesus. Shout it from the rooftops, live it out in your daily life, and watch as He transforms not only your own heart but the hearts of those around you.

Remember, Jesus is not just another way; He is the way, the truth, and the life (John 14:6). And that, my friends, is the biggest deal of all.

Jesus isn't just another name; He's the name above all names. In a world full of distractions, let's remember that Jesus is the biggest deal of all.

"Therefore, God elevated him to the place of highest honor and gave him the name above all other names."
—Philippians 2:9

CHAPTER 5

LOUDER THAN WORDS

HAVE YOU EVER felt stuck in your spiritual journey, wondering how to take the next step? I've been there, more times than I care to admit, but I want to share with you a powerful truth that can transform your life: the fastest way to get unstuck is to find a way to serve others.

You see, there's often a disconnect between what we say we believe and what we live out. We may profess our faith with our lips, but if we really want to know what's in our hearts, we need to look at how we're living. As the apostle Paul wrote in 1 Corinthians 13:5, "[Love] does not behave rudely, does not seek its own, is not provoked, thinks no evil..."

So, what does serving have to do with taking the next step in growing our faith?

Everything.

Jesus Himself made it crystal-clear in Mark 10:43 when He said, "Whoever wants to become great among you must be your servant." Just like in a children's classroom, we 'show-and-tell' our willingness to love others to a degree of naturally serving them. Our actions speak louder than our words.

When we connect the verse from 1 Corinthians with the idea of serving, we discover that as we love, we will serve. Service without love can be good, but service **because we love** is a powerful experience. This verse talks about **what love does**. If we really love others, not just in words but in action, it will show. In fact, if we love God, He will give us plenty of opportunities to serve other folks and live as leaders in His greatness.

The 'love passage' in 1 Corinthians 13: 4–7 paints a beautiful picture of what God's kind of love looks like. It tells us that love does not behave rudely. That means, you don't treat others as less than yourself or as though you are greater than them. When we serve out of love rather than duty, it's perfectly apparent. To serve out of love is the greatness of Christ working in and through us.

Love keeps its cool, even in the face of adversity.

The passage also says that love is not provoked. It doesn't pop off in a fit of anger or 'lose it' with folks just because things don't go your way. Love keeps its cool, even in the face of adversity.

Finally, love thinks no evil. It doesn't assume the worst about people or suspect them of having an agenda to hurt you. I once read a study that claimed, we find something wrong with others seven times before we find one thing we approve of. But you see, we don't serve others because of their need; we serve others because we are simply following the way of Jesus.

At its core, loving others means that we don't just react or respond with what feels right in the moment. It requires an adjustment to our attitude. But if you really choose to serve others out of your love for God and your love for others, you are truly great in the eyes of the Lord. Rather than just doing what feels good, you can learn to let the love of God that is in your heart come out. When you do, you'll be a light for Jesus in ways you've only imagined!

So, my friend, I encourage you to open your eyes and look for opportunities to serve others today. Choose to act and respond out of love, rather than selfishness. Choose to live like Jesus and experience the blessing found in service.

I know it's not always easy. We live in a world that tells us to put ourselves first, to look out for number one. But that's not the way of Jesus. He came not to be served, but to serve, and to give His life as a ransom for many (Mark 10:45). When we follow in His footsteps, when we choose to serve others out of love, we discover the joy and fulfillment that can only be found in Him.

It might start with something small, like offering to help a neighbor with their groceries or listening to a friend who's going through a tough time. But as you make serving others a habit, as you let the love of God flow through you, you'll find that it becomes a natural part of who you are. You'll start to see opportunities to serve everywhere you go, and you'll experience the blessing of being used by God to make a difference in the lives of others.

I'll never forget the first time I visited a nursing home to spend time with the residents there. I was nervous at first, not knowing what to expect. But as I sat and talked with those precious people, as I listened to their stories and held their hands, I felt the love of God welling up inside me. I realized that I wasn't just serving them; I was serving

Jesus Himself. And in that moment, I experienced joy and a sense of purpose that I had never known before.

That's the power of serving others. It's not just about doing good deeds or checking off a box on our spiritual to-do list. It's about allowing the love of God to transform us from the inside out, to shape us into the image of Christ. It's about discovering the greatness that comes not from seeking our own glory, but from laying down our lives for the sake of others.

So, let me ask you: what's holding you back from serving others today? Is it fear, pride, or simply not knowing where to start? Whatever it is, I want to encourage you to take that first step. Ask God to show you how you can love and serve those around you. Trust that He will give you the strength and the courage you need to follow through.

And as you do, you'll find that serving others isn't just the key to getting unstuck in your spiritual growth; it's the key to experiencing the abundant life that Jesus came to give us. It's the key to discovering the joy, the peace, and the purpose that can only be found in Him.

So, my friend, **choose to live like Jesus and experience the blessing found in service.** Choose to love others not just in words, but in action. Choose to let the light of Christ shine through you in a world that desperately needs His love. It could be the very thing that helps you move forward.

The fastest way to get unstuck in your
spiritual journey is to serve others.
Actions speak louder than words, so
let your faith be seen, not just heard.

*"Dear children, let's not merely say that we love
each other; let us show the truth by our actions."*
—1 John 3:18

46

CHAPTER 6

AUTHORITY IS NOT A 4-LETTER WORD

WHAT IF THE reason you're stalled is because you're fighting with God? I guess it's okay to fight with God, as long as you know that you won't win!

"Everyone must submit to governing authorities. For all authority comes from God, and those in positions of authority have been placed there by God." (Romans 13:1)

As a young and ambitious ninth grader, I had the privilege of starting on my high school football team. My coach, Bobby Johnson, entrusted me with the high honor of stepping into the role as our long snapper. In those days, players never came off the field. I played linebacker on defense, fullback on offense, and was the long snapper for punts and extra points. Coach Johnson gave me instructions that I, in my youthful arrogance, received as mere gentle suggestions. Just in case you are wondering, nothing was subtle about Bobby Johnson. I took it upon my 15-year-old self to do the exact opposite of his instruction. It seemed so right to me at the time! Needless to say, it was a disaster, and I ran the steps of the stadium until I threw my guts up. This experience taught me a valuable lesson: being accountable includes obeying your superiors.

Throughout my life, I've also had plenty of opportunities to follow the direction of the Divine, but instead, I've gone in the opposite direction and, you guessed it, faced disastrous results. It's a common struggle, to respect and submit to authority figures, especially when they drive us nuts, seem out of touch, or appear undeserving of our respect due to their actions. Your co-workers might not recognize your incredible gifts, or your supervisor might come down on you hard. However, the Scriptures give us no pass on accountability.

Following direction and being under authority isn't for the faint of heart. It can be one of the hardest things you do. It takes character, grit, and a lot of positive attitude adjustments to respect those you are accountable to. But we're challenged in Scripture to respect and be accountable to those in authority over us, regardless of our personal feelings or opinions.

> It takes character, grit, and a lot of positive attitude adjustments to respect those you are accountable to.

The Scriptures never tell us to respect only those who understand us or those who seem worthy of our respect. It tells us to respect those in positions of authority. Period!

Respect means not trashing them behind their back, even when you disagree with their decisions or feel they are undeserving of their position. Respect means choosing to display a good attitude, even when you don't understand or agree with a decision or order. Respect means responding to those over you with the Divine's love, whether you think that they deserve it or not.

It's essential to understand that respecting authority doesn't mean blindly following orders or compromising your values. It also doesn't mean that you should tolerate abuse or enable sinful behavior. There may be times when you need to respectfully voice concerns or stand up against injustice. For potentially dangerous or harmful situations, or if an authority figure is engaging in illegal, unethical, or abusive practices, it is crucial to seek help and take appropriate action through proper channels. God does not condone the misuse of authority or the mistreatment of others. However, in most everyday situations, showing respect and submission to authority is crucial for maintaining order, fostering unity, and ultimately, pleasing God.

The Bible provides numerous examples of individuals who chose to respect authority, even in challenging circumstances. Daniel, despite being taken captive and living in a foreign land, showed respect to his superiors while remaining faithful to God (Daniel 1:8–16). David, even when faced with the opportunity to harm King Saul, who was unjustly pursuing him, chose to honor Saul's authority as God's anointed (1 Samuel 24:6–7). These examples demonstrate that respecting authority is not always easy, but it is the right thing to do.

Moreover, respecting authority is not just about outward compliance; it's about cultivating a heart of submission and humility. In Ephesians 6:5–8, Paul instructs servants to obey their earthly masters with sincerity of heart, as unto Christ, knowing that their ultimate reward comes from God. This principle applies to all of us, regardless of our position in life. When we choose to respect authority, we are ultimately submitting to God and acknowledging His sovereignty over all aspects of our lives.

In our daily lives, we can demonstrate respect for authority in various ways. At work, this means following company policies, completing tasks assigned by supervisors, and maintaining a positive attitude, even when faced with challenges or disagreements. In our families, it means honoring our parents, even as adults (Ephesians 6:1–3) and submitting to one another in love (Ephesians 5:21). In our interactions with government officials and law enforcement, it means obeying laws and showing respect, even when we disagree with certain policies or decisions (1 Peter 2:13–17).

Ultimately, respecting authority is about trusting God and His divine plan. When we submit to those in authority over us, we are acknowledging that God has placed them in their positions for a reason, even if we don't always understand why. By choosing to respect authority, we align ourselves with God's will and open ourselves up to His blessings and favor.

Push yourself to speak well of those in authority over you. Choose, with great intentionality, to love them even when they feel unlovable. Choose to be a person of character and respect the people in authority over you. When you do, you will discover that God will bless you in a way that makes no sense in your humanity, but perfect sense in God's divinity.

As you navigate the challenges of submitting to authority, remember that you are not alone. Lean on God's strength, wisdom, and guidance. Surround yourself with a community of believers who can encourage and support you in your efforts to live a life of respect and accountability. And when you falter, as we all do at times, seek forgiveness and grace, both from those in authority and from God Himself.

In a world that often celebrates rebellion and individualism, choosing to respect authority may seem countercultural. But as followers of Christ, we are called to be set apart, to be a light in the darkness, and to demonstrate the love and character of God in all that we do. By embracing the challenge of respecting authority, we can be powerful witnesses for Christ and experience the abundant life He has promised us.

God created you to live under authority. Honor God as you honor those in authority in your life!

CHAPTER 7

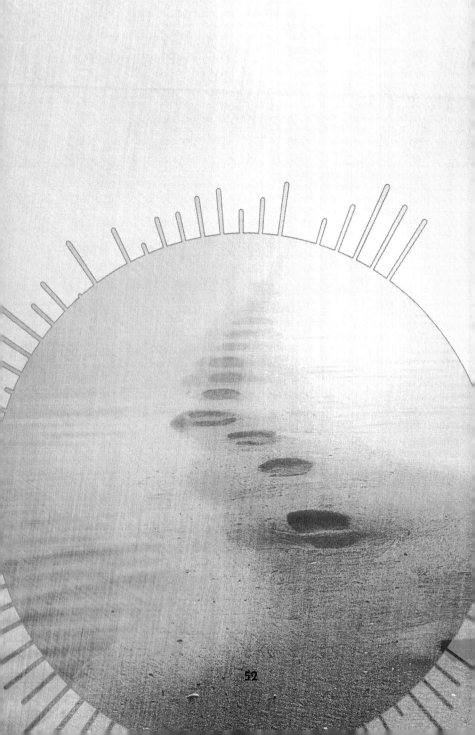

WALKING IN THE SPIRIT OF GOD

YOU'VE PROBABLY HEARD the phrase, "walking in the Spirit of God." It sounds noble, almost lofty, and it's something preachers say with conviction. But for many of us, it's a phrase that remains shrouded in mystery. Our spiritual growth becomes more natural when we learn how to walk in the Spirit. Everything we've talked about so far becomes a little easier when we learn to rely on the Spirit.

How do we make walking in the Spirit of God happen?

How do we truly walk in the Spirit of God?

Growing up in church, many of us were told about the Holy Spirit. Yet, we were almost afraid to mention Him, perhaps due to the overemphasis on control within the church. There was a fear that those who fully embraced the Spirit of God were a bit too radical and a bit too unpredictable. We were taught to be cautious and to keep things orderly, and sometimes, that meant relegating the Holy Spirit to the background.

Years ago, I remember preaching at a church nearby. During the service, a lady was belting out a solo that was simply phenomenal. Enthralled, I found myself clapping and raising my hands in worship. I looked around and realized I was the only one. After the service, the chairman of the deacons made a beeline for me. He reprimanded me for clapping and raising my hands, saying it was against their decorum. In that moment, I realized just how uncomfortable we are with freely expressing our spirituality.

But here's the truth: walking in the Spirit of God isn't about being wild or uncontrolled; it's about allowing God to lead us, to guide us, to fill us with His presence. It's about surrendering our need for control and letting God take charge.

THE PROMISE OF THE HOLY SPIRIT

In Galatians 5:16, Paul says, "So I say, let the Holy Spirit guide your lives. Then you won't be doing what your sinful nature craves." This verse highlights a critical point: we have two natures within us. When we accept Christ, we receive not only salvation but also the gift of the Holy Spirit. Jesus promised to leave us a Helper, a Comforter, and a Counselor—the Spirit of God.

This Spirit is not a distant entity but a present reality in our lives. He's our guide, our strength, and our helper in times of need. The struggle, however, is real. Our sinful nature is constantly at war with the Spirit. The desires of our flesh pull us one way, while the Spirit pulls us another. It's a battle, and it's one that we need to be aware of if we are to walk in the Spirit.

THE BATTLE

There is an internal battle inside of us. Galatians 5:17 says, "The sinful nature wants to do evil, which is just the opposite of what the Spirit wants. And the Spirit gives us desires that are the opposite of what the sinful nature desires." These two forces are constantly fighting each other. The challenge is to align our will with the Spirit and not the flesh.

Our sinful nature craves things that are contrary to God's will. Paul lists these in Galatians 5:19–21, things like sexual immorality, impurity, jealousy, outbursts of anger, and selfish ambition. These are the weeds in our garden that choke out the good fruit God wants to produce in us. The good news is that when we allow the Spirit to lead us, He produces a different kind of fruit in our lives.

> The good news is that when we allow the Spirit to lead us, He produces a different kind of fruit in our lives.

THE CHOICE

We do have options. When faced with the choice between our sinful nature and the Spirit, we must decide ahead of time to choose character over convenience. In Galatians 5:22–23, Paul describes the fruit of the Spirit: love, joy, peace, patience, kindness, goodness, faithfulness, gentleness, and self-control. These qualities are evidence of the Spirit's work in our lives.

Think about it like a garden. If we don't tend to our garden, weeds will overrun it. But if we nurture it, water it, and care for it, we will see beautiful fruit. The same is true in our spiritual lives. We need to actively say "yes" to the Spirit and "no" to our flesh. It's a daily decision, a moment-by-moment choice to let the Spirit lead.

The distance between our head and our heart is what often keeps us from walking in the Spirit. Our minds can be logical, skeptical, and resistant, while our hearts long for God. The key to bridging this gap is a simple three-letter word: yes.

When we say "yes" to the Spirit, we open ourselves up to God's best for us. It's a surrender, a submission to His will and His ways.

Saying "yes" to the Spirit might mean stepping out of our comfort zones, raising our hands in worship, or speaking out when we feel prompted. It's about letting go of control and trusting that God knows best. It's about letting the wind of the Spirit blow through our lives, filling our sails, and taking us where He wants us to go.

THE VICTORY

When we walk in the Spirit, we can expect opposition from our flesh. But we can also expect to overcome. In John 15:5, Jesus says, "Yes, I am the vine; you are the branches. Those who remain in me, and I in them, will produce much fruit. For apart from me you can do nothing." Walking in the Spirit is about remaining connected to Jesus, the source of our strength and the giver of life.

It's not about trying harder or being better. It's about allowing the Spirit to work in us and through us. It's about yielding to His promptings and trusting in His power. The

Spirit gives us the strength to stand, the courage to speak, and the grace to love. He produces in us that which we cannot produce on our own.

PRACTICAL STEPS TO WALKING IN THE SPIRIT

1. **Get in the Bible:** Psalm 119:105 says, "Your word is a lamp to guide my feet and a light for my path." The Bible is our guidebook and our manual for life. Read it, meditate on it, and let it shape your thinking.

2. **Pray Often:** 1 Thessalonians 5:17 says, "Never stop praying." Prayer is our lifeline to God. It's how we communicate with Him and how we align our hearts with His. Make prayer a regular part of your day.

3. **Clean Up Your Life:** 1 John 1:9 says, "But if we confess our sins to him, he is faithful and just to forgive us our sins and to cleanse us from all wickedness." Confession is about acknowledging our sins and turning away from them. It's about pulling up the weeds in our garden and allowing God to plant good fruit.

4. **Hang Out with Other Believers:** Hebrews 10:25 says, "And let us not neglect our meeting together, as some people do, but encourage one another, especially now that the day of his return is drawing near." Community is important. Surround yourself with people who will encourage you and hold you accountable.

57

5. **Give Up Control:** Romans 12:1 says, "And so, dear brothers and sisters, I plead with you to give your bodies to God because of all he has done for you. Let them be a living and holy sacrifice—the kind he will find acceptable. This is truly the way to worship him." Surrender your life to God and let Him lead and guide you.

We'll find that walking in the Spirit is not only possible but also incredibly fulfilling.

Walking in the Spirit of God isn't a one-time event. It's a daily journey, a continual process of saying "yes" to God and "no" to our flesh. It's about yielding to His leadership, trusting in His power, and allowing Him to produce His fruit in our lives.

Remember the quote from A.W. Tozer: "The spirit-filled life is not a special deluxe edition of Christianity. It is part and parcel of the total plan of God for His people." The Spirit of God isn't an add-on or an extra. He's essential to living the life God has called us to.

We'll talk more about the Spirit later. For now, let's step into the garden of our lives. Let's tend to it with care, pulling up the weeds and nurturing the fruit. Let's say "yes" to the Spirit and allow Him to lead us. And as we do, we'll find that His presence brings peace, joy, and a deep sense of purpose. We'll find that walking in the Spirit is not only possible but also incredibly fulfilling. And we'll see the fruit of His work in our lives, drawing others to the beauty of a life surrendered to God. That, my friend, is real growth.

Walking in the Spirit isn't just for the spiritual elite—it's for every believer. Let's rely on His guidance and watch as our faith journey becomes more natural and empowered.

"Since we are living by the Spirit, let us follow the Spirit's leading in every part of our lives."
—GALATIANS 5:25

CHAPTER 8

⟫

ACTIVE OBEDIENCE

HAVE YOU EVER found yourself at a crossroads, wondering what God's plan is for your life? Perhaps you've been asking, "What should I do?" or "Where should I go?" If so, you're not alone. These are the number one questions I hear from folks who seek my counsel.

I want to assure you that God doesn't play hide and seek with His design and destination for your life. He has a beautiful plan for you, a plan to prosper you and give you hope and a future (Jeremiah 29:11). The challenge lies not in God's communication, but in our own hearing and answering of His voice.

I know this from firsthand experience. Years ago, a dear friend, Terry Herald, asked me if I had ever considered serving the local church in full-time ministry. Terry saw something in me that I had not yet recognized in myself. Before I knew it, I was sitting with a personnel team, considering a role as a staff member at a large church.

My initial response was, "No thanks!" I couldn't imagine making such a low salary, so I turned down the offer without even praying about it. That's when I embarked on a journey that I never want to replay—a journey remarkably similar to Jonah's.

In the Bible, we read about Jonah, a man who was told by God to go to the godless city of Nineveh and preach the message of the Holy God of Israel. Like me, Jonah said, "No thanks!" and caught a boat heading in the opposite direction. As a result, he found himself amid a terrible storm that threatened to sink the ship and take the lives of all on board.

Time and time again, He sent warning shots across my bow, but I ignored them or, worse yet, headed in the opposite direction.

While I didn't experience a literal storm at sea, I faced storms of financial, relational, and familial disasters. Everything I touched seemed to fall apart, even ventures that had previously been successful. Relationships crumbled, and family challenges felt like waves threatening to drown me. I was experiencing the consequences of active disobedience.

You see, I had known since the age of fifteen that I was called to serve the church and surrender my life to the Gospel ministry. But my goals were all financial. I wanted money and fame, and for a season, the Lord allowed my disobedience. Time and time again, He sent warning shots across my bow, but I ignored them or, worse yet, headed in the opposite direction.

Here's the lesson, my friend: The calling of God is no greater to vocational ministry than it is to real estate, law, military, or insurance. It's not about the specific role; it's about our obedience to His direction. I knew what I was supposed to do, but I delayed the response that He demanded. He required active obedience from me.

Like Jonah, I tried to throw off the extra weight, blame something else, or hide from God. And, like Jonah, I failed miserably. It wasn't until I finally said, "Lord, it's me. I'm sorry," that things began to change.

You see, partial obedience or delayed obedience is, essentially, total disobedience. And total disobedience will always lead to heartache, sorrow, and failure. I experienced all that firsthand. But the good news is that the moment I answered God's call, He wrapped His arms around me and warmed my soul with the affection of a perfect, loving Heavenly Father.

If you find yourself wondering where to go or what to do, I want to share four steps that can help you avoid the "Jonah Syndrome"—steps I wish I had taken all those years ago:

1. **Don't just pray: hush and listen.** God's voice is crystal clear when we spend the right amount of time with Him.

2. **Seek godly counsel** from those who have nothing to gain from your decision and prayers.

3. **Build a Christ-honoring routine into your daily life.** When we experience Scripture, prayer, gratitude, and quietude as part of our daily rhythm, we are more prone to hear and respond to the direction of the Divine.

4. **Don't walk timidly in the direction of the Divine, run boldly.** I guarantee you that He will be cheering you on!

In the end, Jonah turned around after spending a few days in the belly of a big fish. He ran to Nineveh, where every person in the city turned to God. In my own story, I've been part of some of the most amazing things since turning around and running to God. I'm still prone to wander, as the old hymn says, but I'm quick to return. And when I do, He is always there with fresh direction and endless grace.

Friend, I don't know what storms you may be facing or what decisions you're wrestling with, but I do know this: God loves you more than you can possibly imagine. He has a plan for your life that is far greater than anything you could devise on your own. And He is always ready to welcome you back with open arms, no matter how far you've strayed.

So, if you find yourself at a crossroads today, I encourage you to take a step of faith. Hush and listen for God's voice. Seek wise counsel from those who love Him. Build a life centered on His Word and His presence. And when you hear His call, don't hesitate, run boldly in the direction of His divine plan.

It won't always be easy. There may be storms along the way and moments when you feel like you're drowning in the waves of life, but I promise you this: God will never leave you or forsake you. He will be with you every step of the journey, guiding you, strengthening you, and cheering you on.

And in the end, when you look back on your life, you'll see that every step of obedience, every moment of surrender, was leading you to a place of greater joy, greater purpose, and greater intimacy with the One who loves you most.

So, my friend, don't be afraid to say "yes" to God. Don't let fear or doubt hold you back from the incredible adventure He has in store for you. Trust in His goodness, lean into His grace, and watch as He takes you places you never dreamed possible.

As the psalmist wrote, "Delight yourself in the Lord, and He will give you the desires of your heart" (Psalm 37:4). When we surrender our lives to Him, when we make Him our greatest delight, He not only guides us but also shapes our desires to align with His perfect will.

This is the beauty of active obedience—it's not about gritting our teeth and doing something we dread. It's about falling more deeply in love with Jesus, about discovering the joy and freedom that come from walking in step with His Spirit.

So, wherever you find yourself today, know that God is with you, He is for you, and He has a plan for your life that is more wonderful than you can possibly imagine.

Take that step of obedience and watch as He unfolds a story that will leave you in awe of His goodness and grace.

CHAPTER 9

BIG TRUST

LIFE CAN BE confusing at times, can't it? We face decisions every day, big and small, and it's not always clear which way to go. But there's a simple, powerful truth that can guide us through even the most challenging of circumstances. It's found in Proverbs 3:5–6:

> *"Trust in the Lord with all your heart; do not depend on your own understanding. Seek his will in all you do, and he will show you which path to take."*

These words have the power to change your life if you let them. Let's take a closer look at what they mean.

1. Trust in the Lord

It all starts with trust. Any real relationship must start with some level of trust. It's the only way a true friendship remains. It's the only way a marriage works. It's the simple reason why an employer hires employees, or why the employees stay employed. **It's all about trust.**

But trusting in the Lord is an entirely new dimension. This is our trust in a divine, eternal, all-powerful, all-loving God. He is worthy of our trust. And the trust is important, not just because of who God is, but because of the way in which we must trust Him: with all our hearts. That involves every fiber of your being. That's the kind of trust we can have in God-a complete, unshakable, deep, abiding trust.

If you have trusted God for salvation, you can trust Him with the rest of your life, too. You can trust him in every single detail because He's got you covered.

2. Don't Lean on Your Understanding

The verse involves a positive, something you must do, which is to trust. But it also involves a negative—something you must not do: "Don't lean on your own understanding."

The verse tells us that we ought not to be self-reliant. Our choices must be founded in our trust in the Divine. Self-reliance is a deceptive trap. We begin to pride ourselves in something: our friends, our looks, our intellect, our religion, our family, whatever. And when we do, it takes away our trust in the Lord. It becomes trust in self.

This is a dangerous place to be, my friend, because our understanding is limited. We can't see the big picture and we don't know what the future holds. But God does. He sees it all, from beginning to end, and He knows what's best for us, even when we don't understand.

3. Instead, Acknowledge God in Everything

The fix to this self-reliance is found in the first command of the verse, "Trust in the Lord with all your heart," which is purposed in the next verse, "In all your ways acknowledge Him" (Proverbs 3:6).

The word "acknowledge" isn't a polite tip of the hat to the 'man upstairs,' or a few words of grace over your meal, or even attendance at church to let Him know we're still cool with what He's doing. It's far more. It's allowing Him control, command, and involvement in all your life—in all your ways.

It means bringing God into every decision, every relationship, and every aspect of your life. It means saying, "God, I trust You. I don't always understand, but I know You're in control. Show me the way."

And when you do that, something amazing happens.

THE RESULT: STRAIGHT PATHS

The verse ends with a promise. He will make your paths straight and paths lead toward a destination, a goal.

So, trusting God in every area of your life gives you a sense of purpose. It indicates that there will be a clear understanding of where you are going and what you are doing. You realize that you are trusting Him and He is making your paths straight. Straight paths include purity, and a pure life means less sinful compromise and more Christlike attitudes, actions, and behaviors. It's a life that honors God and blesses others.

He will make your paths straight and paths lead toward a destination, a goal.

This is the kind of life that God promises and it's the kind of life that you can have. But it begins with trust and acknowledging God in every way.

I know it's not always easy. There are times when trusting God feels like stepping off a cliff into the unknown. But

I promise you, my friend, He will catch you and He will guide you. He will never let you down.

I've seen it in my own life, repeatedly. When I've trusted God, even when I didn't understand, He has always come through. He has always made my paths straight. And He wants to do the same for you.

So, whatever you're facing today, whatever decisions you're wrestling with, I encourage you to trust in the Lord with all your heart and to not lean on your own understanding. Acknowledge Him in everything and watch as He guides your steps, day by day, moment by moment, leading you into the abundant life He has planned for you.

It's a journey of faith; a journey of trust. But it's a journey worth taking because when you trust in the Lord, when you acknowledge Him in all your ways, you'll discover a peace, a purpose, and a joy that you never knew possible.

So, take that step today. Trust in the Lord and let Him guide your path.

Live in big trust today!

When life gets confusing, remember:
Trust in God, not in your own
understanding. He will guide your path
when you place your trust in Him.

*"Trust in the Lord with all your heart;
do not depend on your own understanding. Seek his will in all you do, and
he will show you which path to take."*
—PROVERBS 3:5-6

CHAPTER 10

THE PAYOFF OF TRUST

ANYTIME WE TRUST God, we reap God-like results. Sometimes, we're tempted to rush and miss the blessing of what we can do in the process of trust. In our fast-paced, ever-changing world, it's easy to get caught up in our own plans and ambitions. We often find ourselves trying to fit God into our lives, rather than the other way around. But here's a thought that could shift your perspective: Instead of attempting to squeeze God into your plans, what if you discovered His plans and fitted your life into them?

One of the most common pitfalls we encounter is trusting God with the big things in our lives while attempting to handle the details on our own. We tend to live from one major event to the next, neglecting the small, everyday moments that shape our character and faith. The problem with this approach is that it stunts our spiritual growth, leaving us perpetually immature.

The secret to growing up spiritually is learning to trust God with the details of your life. It's a simple concept, but one that requires a profound shift in our thinking and actions.

So, here's the question I want you to consider: Do you trust that the One who knows you best knows what's best for your life?

There are at least five positive results of trusting God with the details of your life. These insights have stuck with me, and I believe they can be transformative for you, too.

Result 1: You experience peace.

"My son, do not forget my teaching, but let your heart keep my commandments; for length of days and years of life, and peace they will add to you." (Proverbs 3:1–2)

Amid newfound freedom, it's easy to forget the lessons you've learned in church, your quiet times, and small groups. Don't let the truth you've gained slip away. Instead, apply it to your life. Allow the knowledge in your head to sink deep into your heart. Why? Because every time you apply God's truth to the details of your life, you experience an increase in His peace.

Result 2: You have relationships that work.

"Do not let kindness and truth leave you; bind them around your neck, write them on the tablet of your heart. So you will find favor and good repute in the sight of God and man." (Proverbs 3:3–4)

Kindness and truth are the foundational elements of every healthy relationship, whether it's with your parents, bosses, friends, or romantic partner. When you allow these qualities to guide your interactions, you find favor with others, your relationships flourish, and you experience less drama.

Result 3: You get to know and do the Will of God.

Your greatest need is to know God's will for your life. What does He want for your career, relationships, and future? Many of you find yourselves at a crossroads, desperately seeking direction.

"Trust in the Lord with all your heart, and do not lean on your own understanding. In all your ways acknowledge him, and he will make your paths straight." (Proverbs 3:5–6)

Don't try to figure it out on your own. No matter how intelligent or capable you may be, there are things about your life that only God knows. When you lean on Him, He will make the path before you clear and straightforward.

> **Your greatest need is to know God's will for your life.**

Result 4: You get to reach your full potential.

"Do not be wise in your own eyes; fear the Lord and turn away from evil. It will be healing to your body, and refreshment to your bones." (Proverbs 3:7–8)

When you trust God with the details, you experience wholeness and completeness. You get to live out the unique design God created you for, reaching your full potential and experiencing the abundant life He promises.

Result 5: It is always for your good.

"My child, don't ignore it when the Lord disciplines you, and don't be discouraged when he corrects you. For the Lord corrects those he loves, just as a father corrects a child in whom he delights." (Proverbs 3:11–12)

Being disciplined or corrected rarely feels pleasant in the moment. It's natural to shy away from correction, much like a child trying to avoid a spanking. However, the word "discipline" in this context means pressure. Because God loves you, He applies pressure to the areas of your life where you need to trust Him more. He takes His finger and points out the details that require your attention and surrender.

This brings us back to the original question: Do you trust that the One who knows you best actually knows what's best for your life?

Is there any area of your life where you're feeling pressure? Could that pressure be God's way of highlighting a detail that needs your trust?

Remember, the secret to a thriving Christian life is trusting God with the details. Every time you do, you reap God-like results.

As you navigate the ups and downs of life, I encourage you to shift your perspective. Instead of trying to fit God into your plans, seek out His plans and fit your life into them. When you do, you'll experience a peace that surpasses understanding, relationships that flourish, and a clear sense of purpose and direction.

Trusting God with the details isn't always easy, but it's always worth it. It requires a daily choice to surrender your will to His, to acknowledge His wisdom and goodness, even when you don't understand the bigger picture.

But as you learn to trust Him more deeply, you'll find that His plans for you are far better than anything you could have imagined on your own. You'll discover a life filled with meaning, purpose, and the joy that comes from walking in step with your Creator.

So, take a moment to reflect on the details of your life. Are there areas where you've been trying to maintain control, rather than surrendering them to God? Are there pressures or challenges that you've been facing alone, instead of bringing them before the Lord?

Today, I invite you to make a conscious choice to trust God with every detail, big and small. Lean on His understanding, seek His will, and watch as He guides your steps and transforms your life in ways you never thought possible.

Remember, you are loved by a God who knows you intimately and desires the very best for you. He is worthy of your trust, and He will never lead you astray.

As you embark on this journey of trusting God with the details, know that you are not alone. You are part of a community of believers who are walking the same path, learning to surrender their lives to the One who holds the universe in His hands.

So, take heart, my friend. Trust God with the details and watch as He unfolds a beautiful story in your life—a story of growth, purpose, and unshakable faith. May you experience the peace, favor, and wholeness that comes from fitting your life into His perfect plan.

Trust Him today, and every day, with all the details of your life. For in His hands, even the smallest moments can become the greatest testimonies of His love and faithfulness.

CHAPTER 11

DEALING WITH LIFE'S BULLIES

THERE ARE CHALLENGES along the journey. In the timeless tale of David and Goliath, we find another powerful reminder of the strength that lies within each of us when we trust in God. This story, cherished by many since childhood, resonates with the truth that no matter how big or intimidating life's challenges may seem, we can overcome them through faith and the power of the Almighty.

David, a young shepherd boy, stood before the towering giant, Goliath, armed not with a sword or spear, but with an unwavering faith in the God of Israel. He had faced lions and bears in the past, and now he faced a new kind of bully—one that struck fear into the hearts of even the bravest soldiers. But David knew something they didn't: he knew the God of all Creation, and he knew that with God on his side, no enemy could stand against him.

It's easy to look at the giants in our lives and feel overwhelmed, just as the Israelites did when they saw Goliath. We may feel small, weak, and ill-equipped to face the challenges that loom before us but like David, we have a secret weapon: a personal connection to the One True God. When we know God and trust in His word, we can conquer our own fears and face any obstacle with courage and confidence.

So, how did David do it? And more importantly, can we do it, too? The answer to both questions lies in the power of faith and the promises of God. David didn't rely on his own strength or skill to defeat Goliath. Instead, he declared boldly, "You come to me with sword, spear, and javelin, but I come to you in the name of the Lord of Heaven's Armies - the God of the armies of Israel, whom you have defied." (1 Samuel 17:45) He knew that the battle belonged to the Lord, and he trusted God to deliver the victory.

He knew that the battle belonged to the Lord, and he trusted God to deliver the victory.

That same faith is available to each one of us. When we have a relationship with God and trust in His promises, we can face life's bullies with the same boldness and assurance that David had. We can look at our challenges from the perspective of God's kingdom, knowing that all the resources of heaven are at our disposal. And we can activate our faith by saying what we want to see happen, just as David did when he declared that he would defeat Goliath and cut off his head.

But it's not always easy to muster that kind of faith, especially when the giants in our lives seem so big and scary. That's where the power of God's word comes in. As 1 John 4:4 reminds us, "...greater is He that is in you than he that is in the world." When we meditate on the promises of God and allow them to take root in our hearts, we begin to see ourselves the way God sees us: as more than conquerors through Christ who loves us.

So, what do you need to conquer today? Whatever it is, know that you have been given the name of Jesus and the power of His word as your spiritual weapons. Activate your faith by speaking what you want to see happen, and then take bold action, trusting that God will go before you and fight on your behalf.

Remember, you have every quality that David had. God designed you to be an overcomer, to face life's challenges with courage and strength. You don't have to fear the bullies of this world because Jesus has already overcome them. Claim that victory for yourself and energize your faith by speaking boldly and acting decisively.

When the battles seem too hard and the giants too big, remember that God is always with you. He will carry you through your days of despair and give you the peace, joy, and fulfillment that you crave. Trust in His unfailing love and watch what He does in and through you.

So, take heart, my friend. Lift your chin, poke out your chest, and claim the victory that is already yours in Christ. Declare, as David did, that you come in the name of the Lord, and that no weapon formed against you shall prosper. Energize your faith, trust in the God who lives within you, and watch as He leads you into a life of purpose, power, and unshakable peace.

Live in peace, knowing that the same God who enabled David to conquer Goliath is with you always, ready to help you overcome every giant you face. With Him on your side, nothing is impossible, and no bully can stand against you. Take hold of that truth, and let it be the foundation of your faith and the source of your strength, now and always.

82

CHAPTER 12

DON'T BE A JERK

I N A WORLD filled with chaos and conflict, it's easy to get caught up in the whirlwind of negativity and forget the simple yet profound truth that relationships matter. As followers of Jesus, we are called to a higher standard—one that requires us to extend kindness, compassion, and forgiveness to others, even when they don't deserve it.

The apostle Paul reminds us in Ephesians 4:32, "Be kind to one another, tenderhearted, forgiving one another, as God in Christ forgave you." These words are not a suggestion, but a directive straight from the heart of God. They challenge us to rise above our natural inclinations and respond to others with the same grace and mercy that we have received from our Heavenly Father.

But let's be honest, it's not always easy to be kind, especially when others are being jerks to us. We've all experienced the frustration of someone cutting in line, gossiping behind our backs, or just plain getting on our nerves for no apparent reason. In those moments, our instinct is to fight back, to give them a taste of their own medicine, to prove that we won't be pushed around or taken advantage of.

However, as followers of Jesus, we are called to a different way of living. We are called to love others, even when they are unlovable. We are called to forgive, even when forgiveness seems impossible. We are called to be kind, even when kindness is the last thing on our minds.

Why? Because that's exactly what Jesus did for us. When we were lost in our sin, rebelling against God and pushing Him away, He didn't respond with anger or vengeance. Instead, He came to earth, took on human form, and willingly sacrificed His life on the cross to pay the penalty for our sins. He extended forgiveness to us, not because we deserved it, but because of His great love for us.

And now, as recipients of that incredible grace, we are called to extend the same kindness and forgiveness to others. It's not always easy, and it certainly doesn't come naturally, but when we remember the depth of God's love for us, when we meditate on the sacrifice that Jesus made on our behalf, it empowers us to love others in a way that defies human logic.

You see, kindness has the power to transform lives. It can soften hearts, break down walls, and open doors for the gospel to be shared. When we choose to respond to others with gentleness and compassion, even in the face of hostility or indifference, we are reflecting the very nature of God Himself.

Of course, this doesn't mean that we become doormats, allowing others to walk all over us or take advantage of our kindness. There are times when boundaries need to be set and tough conversations had. But even in these moments, we can approach others with a spirit of humility and grace, seeking to understand their perspective and extend forgiveness whenever possible.

And here's the beautiful thing: When we choose to be kind and forgive, even in the face of adversity, we are not only impacting the lives of those around us, but we are also experiencing the joy and freedom that comes from living in obedience to God. We discover the truth that relationships matter, and that the way we treat others has eternal significance.

And who knows? Your kindness may just be the very thing that breaks through someone's hardened exterior and opens their heart to the transforming power of the gospel.

So, the next time someone cuts you off in traffic, gossips about you behind your back, or just plain gets on your nerves, take a deep breath and remember the words of Ephesians 4:32. Choose to be kind. Choose to forgive. Choose to love others the way that Christ has loved you.

It won't always be easy, and there will be times when you fail. But as you continue to seek God's heart and rely on His strength, you will find yourself growing in grace and compassion, becoming more and more like Jesus with each passing day.

And who knows? Your kindness may just be the very thing that breaks through someone's hardened exterior and opens their heart to the transforming power of the gospel. Your forgiveness may be the catalyst that leads to reconciliation and restoration in a broken relationship. Your love may be the light that pierces through the darkness and points others to the hope that can only be found in Christ.

So don't be a jerk. Choose kindness. Choose forgiveness. Choose to value relationships above all else and watch as God uses your obedience to transform lives and bring glory to His name.

86

CHAPTER 13

GROWING UP IN CHRIST

HAVE YOU EVER felt stuck in your spiritual life? Like you're spinning your wheels, not really getting anywhere, but not sure how to move forward? If so, you're not alone. Many struggle with this feeling of spiritual stagnation. We know we should be growing in our faith, but we're not quite sure how to make that happen.

That's where spiritual disciplines come in. Now, I know what you're thinking, "Spiritual disciplines sound about as exciting as watching paint dry," am I right? But stick with me here, because these practices are the key to experiencing the rich, fulfilling life in Christ that we all long for.

Think of it this way: God is always in the same place. He's constant and unchanging. So, when we feel distant from Him, guess who moved? That's right, we did. Our job, then, is to keep moving closer to God and spiritual disciplines are the practices that help us do just that.

Picture a continuum with "far from God" on one end and "close to God" on the other. Where are you on the continuum right now? Be honest with yourself. The goal of spiritual disciplines is to keep moving us along that continuum, closer and closer to God.

Now, here's the thing: we're all at different places on this continuum. Some haven't even taken one step, which means they don't know Jesus yet. And others trusted Christ years ago but haven't grown much since then. We're still spiritual babies, drinking milk when we should be chowing down on steak.

Wherever you are, know this: God wants you to keep growing. He's not content for you to stay where you are. He wants you to mature in your faith, to become more and more like Jesus. As Hebrews 6:1–3 says:

> So let us stop going over the basic teachings about Christ again and again. Let us go on instead and become mature in our understanding. Surely we don't need to start again with the fundamental importance of repenting from evil deeds and placing our faith in God. You don't need further instruction about baptisms, the laying on of hands, the resurrection of the dead, and eternal judgment. And so, God willing, we will move forward to further understanding.

Did you catch that? God wants us to move forward, to grow up in our faith. But here's the key: while only God can truly sanctify us (that is, make us more like Christ), we have a part to play, too. We can cooperate with God in this process of spiritual growth by practicing spiritual disciplines.

Now, I know what some of you are thinking, "But, I'm just so busy. I don't have time for all this spiritual stuff." Let me challenge you on that. If you have time for Netflix, you have time for Jesus. If you have time for social media, you have time for Jesus. It's not about having more time; it's about prioritizing the time you have.

You see, the Christian life is meant to be one of continued growth. Getting saved is just the starting point. It's awesome to know we're going to heaven, but God wants us to experience a taste of heaven right here and now. He wants us to know His peace, His joy, His purpose for our lives. And the way we tap into that is through spiritual disciplines.

So, what do these disciplines look like? Let me give you a practical example. It takes less than seven minutes a day, but it can revolutionize your spiritual life. Here's what you do:

1. Think of one thing you're grateful for and express it to God.

2. Read a short passage of Scripture.

3. Reflect on what God might be saying to you through that passage.

4. Think of an attribute God wants you to embody today (like patience, kindness, etc.).

5. Rate yourself on how well you're doing with that attribute.

6. Pray, asking God for wisdom and courage to live out what He's shown you.

That's it. Simple, right? But if you do this consistently, day after day, it will transform your spiritual life. Because here's the thing: we don't need more intensity in our spiritual lives, we need more consistency.

It's like working out. You're not going to get in shape by exercising intensely for one day and then doing nothing for the rest of the month. You'll see much better results from exercising a little bit every day. The same is true in our spiritual lives.

Now, let me be clear: the goal aren't the disciplines themselves. The goal is to love God more. These practices are just tools to help us grow closer to Him. They're not about earning God's love or impressing others. They're about nurturing our relationship with God.

When we consistently practice spiritual disciplines, three things happen:

1. We build consistency in our spiritual lives.

2. We prevent complacency.

3. We draw closer to God.

Let's talk about that second point for a moment. Complacency is a real danger in our spiritual lives. It's that attitude that says, "I'm fine where I am. I don't need to grow." But here's the truth: if you're not moving forward in your faith, you're sliding backward. There's no standing still in the Christian life.

Drawing closer to God is what it's all about. Jesus said in John 15:5, "I am the vine; you are the branches. If you remain in me and I in you, you will bear much fruit; apart from me you can do nothing." The closer we stay to Jesus, the more our lives will reflect His character. We'll start to see the fruit of the Spirit, love, joy, peace, patience, kindness, goodness, faithfulness, gentleness, and self-control, growing in our lives.

Now, I know some of you are thinking, "But I've got the Holy Spirit. Can't He just do all this for me?" Well, yes, the Holy Spirit could. But here's the thing: He's waiting for you to cooperate with Him. It's like He's standing there saying, "I'm ready when you are. Just turn me loose in your life!"

The closer we stay to Jesus, the more our lives will reflect His character.

So, how do we do that? How do we 'turn loose' the Holy Spirit in our lives? The answer is: By consistently practicing spiritual disciplines. By making time each day to connect with God through His Word and prayer. By cultivating an attitude of gratitude. By serving others in Jesus' name.

I'll be honest with you: I wish I had taken spiritual disciplines seriously in my 20s, but I didn't really get serious about them until my 50s. I'm 64 now, and let me tell you, I can't imagine how much more secure I'd be in my faith today if I'd started earlier. I can't imagine the blessings I've missed because I lived on my self-sufficiency for so long.

When I became the pastor at Sugar Hill Church in 2011, I was the single biggest jerk on the planet. I was certain I knew everything. I knew what to do, how to do it, and how to grow the church. You know what I realized? I didn't know jack. God had to humble me, to show me how much I needed Him. And He's still doing that work in me because I still struggle with self-sufficiency and pride.

But here's the beautiful thing: God can use anyone who's willing to grow, to learn, to keep moving closer to Him. I am the least capable preacher I know, and I am the last person I would have chosen to pastor a church. And yet, by simply inserting spiritual disciplines into my life, God has been able to use me in ways I never could have imagined.

My life story is pretty whacked out. There's nothing in my background that qualifies me to do what I do—nothing except this one thing: "Lord, I want to know you more, I want to love you more, and I want to lead others to do the same." When that becomes the cry of your hearts, God will do amazing work in you, through you, and for you.

So, here's my challenge to you: decide today to become a healthy keeper of your soul. Choose to grow up in your faith, stop drinking spiritual milk, and start chowing down on the meat of God's Word. Stop whining like spiritual toddlers and start maturing into the men and women God has called you to be.

It's not always easy. Growing pains hurt but I promise you, it's worth it. The peace, the joy, the sense of purpose that comes from a deep, growing relationship with God—there's nothing else like it in the world. So, what's holding you back? Are you too busy? Make time. Are you afraid? Take a step of faith. Are you comfortable where you are? Remember that complacency is the enemy of growth.

Whatever it is, I urge you to push past it. Start small, if you need to, by trying the seven-minute exercise I mentioned earlier. Download a Bible app and start a short reading plan, listen to a Christian podcast on your commute instead of sports radio. Find a way to serve others in Jesus' name.

Just do something. Take one step and then another, and another. Before you know it, you'll find yourself moving along that continuum, growing closer to God, becoming more like Jesus.

Remember, God's not looking for perfection, He's looking for progress. He's not demanding overnight transformation; he's inviting you into a lifelong journey of growth and discovery. What do you say? Are you ready to grow up in Christ? Are you ready to experience all that God has for you? Are you ready to move from spiritual milk to spiritual meat?

The choice is yours. God is ready and waiting. He's got blessings in store for you that you can't even imagine but you've got to take the first step. Will you do it? Will you commit today to growing in your faith? To practicing spiritual disciplines? To becoming the mature believer God has called you to be?

I pray you will because I promise you, there's no adventure more exciting, no journey more fulfilling, than growing up in Christ.

94

CHAPTER 14

CLOSE

WHEN I THINK back to my middle school days, my best friends were Barry, Zach, and Jared. We were inseparable. We lived in the same neighborhood and did virtually everything together. We rode to school together, hung out at each other's houses, and had countless adventures. Barry's house was the ultimate hangout spot, with a barn built by his dad that served as our personal playground. We'd climb the rafters, goof off, and create memories that, at the time, felt like they'd last a lifetime.

But, as life often reveals, things change. Despite our best efforts to stay connected, the close-knit friendship we once shared slowly drifted apart. It's a common experience, one that many of us can relate to. Think about your own middle school friends, the ones who once occupied the center of your world. How many of them are still a significant part of your life today? How many would you still consider your best friends?

More often than not, the answer is: not many. And it's not necessarily due to a falling out or a big fight. Instead, it's a gradual drifting apart, a natural consequence of life's ever-changing seasons.

Now, let's shift our focus to your relationship with God. Have you ever felt a similar sense of distance or disconnection from Him? Have you felt like you used to be closer to God, but now, for reasons you can't quite pinpoint, that closeness has faded?

As human beings, we all long for connection, for the reassurance that someone truly knows us, likes us, and cares for us. In theory, the idea of being close to God seems incredibly appealing. It's a comforting thought, one that promises a deep, meaningful relationship with our Creator. However, in practice, the prospect of actually developing that closeness can be intimidating.

- We might worry that if we get too close to God, He'll ask us to do something we don't want to do, something that goes against our own desires or plans.

- We might fear that drawing near to God will require us to give up all the fun and enjoyment in our lives, resigning ourselves to a life of misery and boredom.

But here's the thing: these fears couldn't be further from the truth. In church, we hear a very different message about God's desires for our lives. We're told that God has incredible plans for us, plans that we don't want to miss out on. We're reminded that God created us to have a real, personal relationship with Him, one that brings joy, purpose, and fulfillment.

Yet, despite these reassurances, we may still harbor a suspicion that there's more to the story, that being close to God is complicated, and that maintaining closeness with Him throughout life is a near-impossible feat. But I'm here to tell you that it's possible. Staying close to God is not only possible but also incredibly rewarding.

Staying close to God is not only possible but also incredibly rewarding.

To illustrate this point, let's look at the story of Abraham, a key figure in the Bible whose journey of faith is found in the book of Genesis. In chapter 12, we're introduced to Abraham (then known as Abram) as God speaks to him for the first time. God instructs Abram to leave his country, his family, and everything he has ever known, and go to a land that God will show him.

What's remarkable about this interaction is that God doesn't simply give Abram a command and then leave him to figure it out on his own. Instead, God continues to speak, offering Abram a glimpse into the incredible future He has in store for him:

> I will make you into a great nation and I will bless you; I will make your name great, and you will be a blessing. I will bless those who bless you, and whoever curses you I will curse; and all peoples on earth will be blessed through you. (Genesis 12:2–3 NIV)

God asked Abram to take a significant step of faith, but before Abram even started on that journey, God wanted him to know that there was a greater plan at work. God wasn't asking Abram to leave his life behind just to make him miserable, but rather to set him on a path toward a life he had never even imagined. God had more in store for Abram, and it all began with a single step of obedience.

Abram's story didn't end there; it was just the beginning. Throughout Abram's life, God continued to walk with him, making promises and giving him increasingly bigger glimpses into the role he would play in the future of God's people. But the point was never simply to get Abram to do more things. Instead, God was continually drawing Abram closer to Himself, building a history and a relationship between them.

As their bond deepened, Abram could look back on all that God had done for him and testify that God is trustworthy and good. Abram learned through experience that God wanted him more than his obedience. This trust allowed Abram to step out in faith, even when God's requests seemed crazy or daunting.

In the same way, God is always drawing you in His direction. He desires a close, personal relationship with you, one built on trust, love, and a shared history. Now, this might sound like good news—and it is! But the real question is: do you believe it's true for you, personally? Do you make decisions based on the belief that God approves of you and wants a relationship with you, or do you find yourself distancing yourself from Him because you think He disapproves?

The truth is, when we truly believe that God wants to be close to us, it changes everything. Imagine how differently you would live if you fully embraced what God says about you. How would your thoughts, actions, and choices be transformed if you trusted in His love and desire for closeness? What if, just for today, you decided to live as if the things God says about you are absolutely true?

And what about your relationship with God? Do you think you'd be more likely to stay close to Him if you trusted in His goodness and unwavering desire to be near you?

So, today I want to encourage you to take a step toward being close to God. When thoughts of guilt or the urge to pull away from Him creep in, choose instead to focus on how He sees you. Choose to believe what He says about you and to trust in the incredible love He demonstrated through His Son, Jesus.

Draw close to God, knowing that He is always drawing close to you. And as you finish reading this devotional, take a moment to ask Him to help you understand the depth of His desire to be close to you.

Remember, staying close to God isn't an impossible task; it's an invitation to experience the fullness of life that He has in store for you. It's an opportunity to build a relationship that will sustain you through every challenge and celebrate with you in every triumph.

So, don't let fear or doubt keep you from the closeness that God is offering. Embrace the journey, trust in His goodness, and watch as your relationship with Him transforms every aspect of your experience.

In the end, staying close to God isn't about following a set of rules or checking off a list of religious duties. It's about accepting His invitation to walk through life with

Him, to trust in His plans, and to experience the incredible love and purpose He has for you.

As you navigate the ups and downs of life, remember that you're never alone. God is always with you, always drawing you closer, and always ready to build a relationship that will change your life in ways you never thought possible.

So, take that step today. Draw close to God and watch as He transforms your journey into an adventure filled with purpose, joy, and the unshakable knowledge that the Creator of the universe deeply loves you.

Just like we stay close to our best
friends, let's stay close to God. When
we walk with Him daily, He shapes our
journey and strengthens our faith.

*"Come close to God, and God
will come close to you."*
—JAMES 4:8

CHAPTER 15

LIVING OUT YOUR FAITH

N TODAY'S WORLD, it seems like drama is everywhere. People are frustrated, ticked off, picking fights, going off, sub tweeting, hacking profiles, and more. It's a crazy reality that we all face, and it's important to acknowledge the obvious truth: in this life, you will face attacks from critics and haters. But here's the good news: you can handle your haters in a holy way.

When faced with opposition and criticism, you have a decision to make. Will you react emotionally, or will you respond appropriately? Before you hit send on that angry message or share your thoughts on social media, I encourage you to consider how the faithful fight back. There is a right way to fight—a holy way to handle your haters.

The story of Daniel in the Bible, specifically in Daniel 6, provides us with a great framework for navigating these challenging situations. Let's dive into three key principles that can help us handle our haters with grace and wisdom.

> There is a right way to fight—a holy way to handle your haters.

1. Expect Opposition

"...these men said, 'We shall not find any ground for complaint against this Daniel unless we find it in connection with the law of his God.'"
(Daniel 6:5, ESV)

One of the first steps in fighting fair is simply realizing that there will be a fight. Opposition is inevitable, especially when God is at work in your life. Here's a simple truth to remember: When God raises you up, expect others to try tear you down.

Daniel experienced this firsthand. He was a man of great success, promoted several times throughout his career. But the higher he rose, the more of a target he became. It's important to be aware of two common characteristics of attacks:

Firstly, you'll often be attacked by someone you know. These attacks can be particularly painful because of the personal connection. It's harder to swallow criticism from a friend or acquaintance than from a mere stranger. This is the nature of it—promotion on the outside often leads to trouble on the inside.

Secondly, attacks frequently come during seasons of success. When things are going well, we tend to let our guard down and live on autopilot. We're not expecting an attack, which makes us more vulnerable. Be careful.

I know attacks aren't fun, but they're going to happen. Opposition often follows obedience. The two go hand in hand. Daniel was promoted and attacked. He was right in the middle of God's will, and yet he still had haters. You've probably been there too, right?

2. Examine Your Options

When the king put a law in place that made it illegal for Daniel to pray, Daniel had to make a choice. He had at least three options:

- He could've stopped praying, if only for a while. After all, he'd been faithful for many years. Would it really hurt if he stopped praying for just a month?

- He could've prayed silently, without people knowing. This way, he'd still maintain his connection with God, just in a more discreet way.

- He could keep praying, just as he had always done, regardless of the consequences.

Going against what would have kept him safe from the authorities, Daniel bravely chose the third option. "When Daniel knew that the document had been signed, he went to his house where he had windows in his upper chamber open toward Jerusalem. He got down on his knees three times a day and prayed and gave thanks before his God, as he had done previously." (Daniel 6:10)

The key here is to make your decision ahead of time to be a person of character. When you haven't decided in advance, it's easy to shift from making decisions based on character to making decisions based on convenience.

My friend, Dave Edwards, talks about this in his book, *LIT: Living Christ's Character from the Inside Out* (2002). He highlights the shift from character to convenience:

> **Character:** I will pray out loud.
> **Convenience:** I don't want to offend anybody.
>
> **Character:** I will make decisions based on God's principles.
> **Convenience:** I will make decisions based on emotions.
>
> **Character:** I will do what God wants.
> **Convenience:** I will do whatever brings pleasure.
>
> **Character:** How will this impact my relationship with God in the future?
> **Convenience:** What seems best now?
>
> **Character:** What does God's Word say?
> **Convenience:** What do others say?
>
> **Character:** I'm going to do the right thing no matter what.
> **Convenience:** I'll do what I want.

Because Daniel chose character, he continued to pray. And here's a powerful truth: bowing to pray gives you the strength to stand. Just as Daniel was able to stand with boldness, so will you when you prioritize your relationship with God.

3. Expect to Overcome

When Daniel chose to keep praying, he didn't know how the story would end. He didn't have a completed Bible to read and know that he would be delivered. But here's what he did know: God had been faithful to him, so he would be faithful to God.

When it comes to how the faithful fight, the key is to decide to do what's right and trust God with the results. And what were the results for Daniel? God delivered him unharmed!

"My God sent his angel, and he shut the mouths of the lions. They have not hurt me, because I was found innocent in his sight. Nor have I ever done any wrong before you, Your Majesty." The king was overjoyed and gave orders to lift Daniel out of the den. And when Daniel was lifted from the den, no wound was found on him, because he had trusted in his God. (Daniel 6:22–23)

So, my friend, I encourage you to respond appropriately before you react emotionally.

So, my friend, I encourage you to respond appropriately before you react emotionally. Remember these three principles:

- When God raises you up, expect others to try to tear you down.

- Bowing to pray gives you the strength to stand and fight.

- Do what's right and trust God with the results.

In a world filled with drama and opposition, it's easy to get caught up in the chaos and lose sight of what really matters. But as followers of Christ, we are called to a higher standard. We are called to handle our haters with grace, wisdom, and unwavering faith.

It's not always easy, and there will be times when the attacks feel overwhelming but remember that you are not alone in this fight. God is with you every step of the way, giving you the strength and courage you need to stand firm in the face of opposition.

So, when the haters come, and they will come, don't be surprised. Expect opposition, but don't let it shake your faith. Instead, use it as an opportunity to draw closer to God, to examine your options, and to choose character over convenience.

And when you do, you'll find that God is faithful. He will guide you, protect you, and give you victory, just as He did for Daniel. You may not always understand His ways, but you can trust His heart. He is for you, and He will never leave you or forsake you.

Stand strong, my friend. Keep praying, keep seeking God's face, and keep doing what's right, no matter what the cost because in the end, this is what it means to fight like the faithful. It's not about winning every battle or silencing every critic. It's about staying true to God, no matter what.

And as you do, you'll find that His grace is sufficient, His power is made perfect in your weakness, and His love will carry you through even the darkest of times.

Don't lose heart and don't give up. Keep fighting the good fight of faith, knowing that the One who is in you is greater than the one who is in the world. And as you do, you'll be a living testament to the power and goodness of God, shining His light in a world that so desperately needs it.

Remember, you are not defined by your haters or your critics. You are defined by your identity in Christ. And in Him, you are more than a conqueror. You are a child of the King, called to live a life of purpose, courage, and unwavering faith. Go forth and fight like the faithful. Trust God, do what's right, and watch as He works all things together for your good and His glory. Know that no matter what comes your way, He will always be with you, always fighting for you, and always lead you in the path of victory.

CHAPTER 16

STAYING PLUGGED IN

HAVE YOU EVER watched the show, *The Amazing Race*? If not, let me give you a quick rundown. It's a competition where pairs of people race around the world, competing against several other teams. The last team to reach each checkpoint is eliminated until only one team remains. Throughout the race, every team inevitably needs to ask for help at some point. There are two primary ways players approach this:

1. Some people ask for help and then take off, trying to figure things out on their own.

2. Others ask for more than just help. They say, "I don't just want you to TELL ME how to get there. I want you to TAKE ME there."

While the second option is clearly more effective, I must admit that the first response often mirrors how I approach my relationship with God. When I find myself in a tough spot—really needing something, in trouble, facing a painful situation, needing to make a big decision quickly, or wanting a big project, event, test, game, or performance to go well—I usually take off running before God can even give me an answer.

Far too often, we treat God as a quick fix; a place we go in big moments when we need fast solutions. But God desires so much more than that. He is not just a cosmic vending machine; He is longs for a deep, meaningful relationship with us. God wants to be the Guide we invite to walk alongside us, not just a GPS we consult for directions.

Jesus beautifully illustrates this concept in a conversation He has with His disciples during their last meal together before His crucifixion. He said, "I am the vine; you are the branches" (John 15:5a, NIV). In their culture, grapevines and branches were common sights because vineyards played a significant role in their society. Jesus refers to Himself as "the vine", which means that He is the source of life for the branches, providing everything they need to survive and thrive.

When we remain plugged into Jesus, He promises that we will "bear much fruit."

Now, unless you frequent the produce section at Kroger, grapevines might not be the most relatable analogy. So, let's put this into a more modern context. Think about the electrical outlets in your room and the devices that rely on them. For a lamp, television, phone charger, video game system, or hair dryer to work, it needs to be plugged into a power source.

In this analogy, the vine is like the electrical outlet—the power source. And just as a vine works in conjunction with its branches, an outlet works hand in hand with an electrical cord. The outlet provides the energy the cord needs to function. The branches, then, are like electrical cords; they need to stay connected to the source to fulfill their purpose.

So, when Jesus says, "I am the vine, you are the branches," He's essentially saying, "I am the outlet, you are the cord."

He continues, "If you remain in me and I in you, you will bear much fruit" (John 15:5b). In other words, Jesus is telling us that the key to a fruitful life is to stay connected to Him, to stay in step with Him. In electrical terms, our main job is to stay plugged in. When we remain plugged into Jesus, He promises that we will "bear much fruit." Just like when an electrical cord is plugged into an outlet, things come to life! The lamp gives light, the cell phone charges, and the game system fires up. In a nutshell, if you want to get the most out of life, stay close to the source of it.

Jesus drives this point home by concluding, "Apart from me you can do nothing" (John 15:5c). Sure, you can try to do everything on your own, and you might even accomplish some impressive things, but you won't bear the fruit that God intends for you unless you stay connected to Him.

Now, it's important to note that getting disconnected doesn't mean you no longer have a relationship with God. It simply means you're missing out on the fullness of life He has in store for you. The great news is that God is always with you and for you. He loves you deeply and wants nothing more than to help you navigate this journey called life.

Remaining connected to God is a habit we can cultivate and a skill we can develop. There are many ways to practice staying plugged in:

- Reading the Bible

- Praying

- Spending time with others who are connected to Him

These are all fantastic ways to "remain" in Him. But for now, let's start with a simple question: "Will you guide me, God?" It's a powerful question to ask at the beginning of the day, before a conversation, before you walk into your house, before you send a text, before a date. Basically, ask God to guide you before any significant moment in your day. It's a way of learning to plug into the source before facing whatever lies ahead.

Remember, God is always looking out for you. He wants you to live a life connected to Him because He knows that's where you'll find the most fulfillment. He understands that if you want to get the most out of life, you need to stay close to the source of it.

So, as you head out today, start here: Ask God to guide you. Stay plugged into the One who wants to bring you to life. Live a life connected to His mission and purpose.

Just like in a race, staying connected
to God gives us the strength
and guidance we need. Don't
just ask for help and run—stay
plugged into His power daily.

"Remain in me, and I will remain in you.
For a branch cannot produce fruit if it
is severed from the vine, and you cannot
be fruitful unless you remain in me."
—JOHN 15:4

THE POWER OF FRIENDS

HAVE A CONFESSION to make: I used to be a serial classroom sleeper. Throughout high school, I prioritized my job over sleep and school, often burning the midnight oil and struggling to stay awake during class. My grades suffered as a result, and I became one of those students who teachers constantly reminded, "If you would just apply yourself..." Deep down, I knew they were right. I had the potential to do better.

Thankfully, things took a turn for the better in college and seminary. I woke up to the realization that simply doing the work made school a lot easier. Groundbreaking, right? As I began to read my assignments and write papers, my grades skyrocketed. I discovered a newfound love for learning, and it transformed my academic experience.

But the truth is, we often find ourselves sleepwalking through life, not just school. We nod off to our potential, getting pulled into what's 'normal' and easy, potentially missing out on our God-given destiny. We miss it because we're asleep, unaware of the incredible plans God has for us.

So, how do we wake up?

While God uses various tools to wake us from our slumber, one of the most powerful is the influence of our friends. The people we spend time with and allow into our lives have a profound impact on who we become.

Consider these well-known phrases, describing the importance of friendships and the role they play in life:

- "It is impossible to live the right life if you have the wrong friends."

- "Show me your friends, and I'll show you your future."

- "Your friends will always determine the quality and direction of your life."

- "Whoever walks with the wise becomes wise, but the companion of fools will suffer harm" (Proverbs 13:20).

God desires to wake you up to your destiny, to the incredible purpose He has for your life. And perhaps, instead of using something to wake you up, God wants to use someone.

I don't mean to sound overly dramatic, but the truth is, you could be just ONE FRIEND AWAY from waking up to your God-given destiny!

However, this won't happen by chance, because not all friendships are created equal. We need intentional, purpose-driven friends in our lives. Take David's life as an example. He had three kinds of friends who helped him wake up to his destiny, and these are the same three types of friends we need to actively pursue.

We need friends that...

1. WAKE US UP TO OUR POTENTIAL.

When God rejected Saul as king, He called Samuel to anoint the next ruler of Israel. As Samuel looked at the candidates presented before him, God repeatedly said, "Nope."

What was going on?

God explained, "People look at the outward appearance, but the Lord looks at the heart" (1 Samuel 16:7). God saw something in David that nobody else could see, and He helped Samuel recognize it, too. In verse 12, God instructs Samuel, "Rise and anoint him; this is the one."

I have a friend like that, a man named PJ Scott, who called me out of the blue just yesterday. He's about 40 years my senior, and when I was a high school student, God used PJ to help me see what God could do in and through my life.

Do you have a friend like that? Someone who helps you live up to your potential in the areas of life that matter most.

2. WAKE US UP TO OUR STRENGTH.

Years later, when Saul sought to kill David out of jealousy and anger over his growing popularity, David found himself on the run, despite his God-given potential.

In this trying time, Saul's own son, Jonathan, stood by David. 1 Samuel 23:15–16 tells us that, "He helped him find strength in God." God used Jonathan to help David find strength when he needed it most. You need a friend like that.

There will be times when you're tempted to give up, when you face challenges that seem insurmountable. In those moments, you need a friend who sticks with you and helps you find the strength to keep standing.

I have a friend named Bryan who stands with me. God brought him into my life at just the right time, when I was tired and overwhelmed, and he helped me find the strength to press on when I didn't think I could.

Do you have a friend like that?

3. WAKE US UP TO TRUTH.

Years later, after David had been king for some time, he took his eyes off the Lord and set them on Bathsheba. He broke God's heart and put the kingdom at risk. For about a year, he didn't think it was a big deal, believing he could cover his sin, until Nathan the prophet showed up.

Nathan told David a story about one man taking advantage of another. David became angry and demanded justice. Then, Nathan simply said to David, "You are that man!" (2 Samuel 12:7).

God used Nathan to help David realize a hard truth that was destroying him. Nathan loved David enough to tell him the truth, waking him up to a reality he had never seen before.

Do you have friends like this? Not just friends you hang out or goof off with, but friends who help you step into the destiny God has for your life.

Don't settle for accidental friendships. Intentionally seek out these kinds of friends, the ones who will challenge you, encourage you, and speak truth into your life. And as my grandmother used to tell me: If you want to have that kind of friend, you must be that kind of friend. Who knows? You might just be the friend who helps someone else realize their God-given destiny.

Would you pray this simple prayer today?

"God, help me to see the people you want in my life. Give me the eyes to see and the heart to be faithful to your leading."

As you navigate the ups and downs of life, remember that the friends you surround yourself with have a profound impact on your journey. They can either help you wake up to your potential, strengthen you in times of weakness, and speak truth into your life, or they can lull you into a state of complacency and compromise.

Choose your friends wisely and be the kind of friend that others need.

Choose your friends wisely and be the kind of friend that others need. Seek out relationships that challenge you to grow, that point you back to God, and that help you become the person He created you to be.

And as you do, trust that God will bring the right people into your life at the right time. He knows the plans He has for you—plans to prosper you and give you hope and a future (Jeremiah 29:11). He will use the friendships He ordains to help you wake up to those plans and walk in the destiny He has for you.

Don't settle for a life of sleepwalking, of missing out on all that God has in store for you. Wake up to your potential, your strength, and the truth of who you are in Christ. Let the friends God places in your life be a catalyst for that awakening and sources of encouragement, accountability, and love.

Remember, you are not alone on this journey. God is with you, and He has surrounded you with a community of believers who are cheering you on, praying for you, and walking alongside you. Embrace those friendships, invest in them, and watch as God uses them to transform your life in ways you never thought possible.

Wake up, my friend. Your destiny awaits. And with God's help and the support of the right friends, you can step into all that He has for you, living a life of purpose, passion, and unshakable faith.

True friends are powerful—
they challenge you to be better
and lift you when you're down.
Surround yourself with people
who push you closer to God.

*"As iron sharpens iron, so a
friend sharpens a friend."*
—PROVERBS 27:17

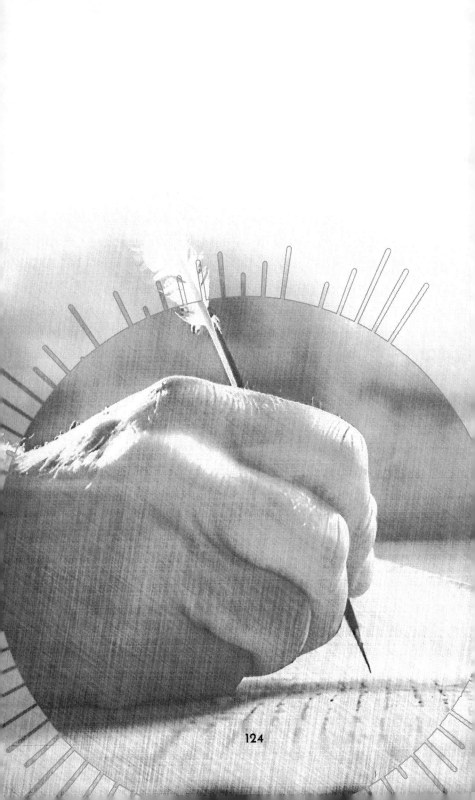

124

CHAPTER 18

YOUR STORY MATTERS

Y EARS AGO, I received a shirt that simply states, "Your Story Matters." The longer I've owned it, the more convinced I've become of the profound truth it conveys.

I firmly believe two things:

- Your story matters.

- You can live a better story.

Every person has a unique and powerful story, and we can gain valuable insights into our own stories by examining the life of Joseph, as recorded in Genesis 37–50.

Here are three essential truths about your story:

1. YOUR STORY HAS A UNIQUE DESIGN (Genesis 37:1-4).

When we first meet Joseph, he is just a teenager. We learn that he is the youngest child in his family and is favored by his father. This favoritism breeds hatred and jealousy among his brothers. Joseph has a dream that foreshadows a day when his entire family will bow down before him. When he shares this dream with his brothers, their hatred intensifies.

Joseph's story had a rough beginning. However, behind the dream was the call and purpose of God for his life. As a teenager, he didn't fully comprehend it, but God had great plans to work through him.

Each of us has a unique call and purpose for our lives. We often discover it by paying attention to the things that frustrate us and break our hearts. Initially, we may not see the big picture, but as we continue to walk with God, our calling becomes clearer.

2. YOUR STORY HAS MANY UPS AND DOWNS (Genesis 37-50).

Joseph's story is full of ups and downs. Here are a few of them:

- ↑ He has a dream.
- ↓ He tells his brothers.
- ↓ He is thrown into a well.
- ↑ He is rescued.
- ↓ He is sold into slavery.
- ↑ He serves in Potiphar's house.
- ↓ He is falsely accused by Potiphar's wife.
- ↑ He meets the cupbearer and baker.
- ↓ The cupbearer forgets him.
- ↑ He stands before Pharaoh.
- ↓ He is reunited with his brothers.

♠ He forgives his brothers.

♠ He saves Egypt.

Your story also has many ups and downs. These fluctuations are not punishment; they are preparation for what God has in store for you. God is far more concerned about developing your CHARACTER than He is about your COMFORT.

3. YOUR STORY CAN BE USED TO SHAPE DESTINY (Genesis 50:15-20).

After their father's death, Joseph's brothers fear that he will seek revenge and punish them for their past actions. They are mistaken.

> When Joseph's brothers saw that their father was dead, they said, 'What if Joseph holds a grudge against us and pays us back for all the wrongs we did to him?' So they sent word to Joseph, saying, 'Your father left these instructions before he died: "This is what you are to say to Joseph: I ask you to forgive your brothers the sins and the wrongs they committed in treating you so badly." Now please forgive the sins of the servants of the God of your father.' When their message came to him, Joseph wept.
> His brothers then came and threw themselves down before him. 'We are your slaves,' they said.
> But Joseph said to them, 'Don't be afraid. Am I in the place of God? You intended to harm me, but God intended it for good to accomplish what is now being done, the saving of many lives.

> *So then, don't be afraid. I will provide for you*
> *and your children.' And he reassured them and*
> *spoke kindly to them. (Genesis 50:15-20, NIV)*

Joseph discovered the redemptive side of his story; after all he had endured, he was able to save the lives of many.

Your story also has a redemptive side. God can use your story as part of His grand narrative to save the lives of many. I encourage you to:

- Fully surrender your life.

- Then, surrender every single day.

Your story matters.

As you navigate the ups and downs of life, remember that each twist and turn serves a purpose in God's grand design. Every challenge you face, every victory you celebrate, and every lesson you learn shapes you into the person God created you to be.

Your story is not just a random series of events; it is a carefully crafted masterpiece, woven together by the loving hands of your Heavenly Father. He sees the beginning from the end, and He knows how each chapter of your life fits into the larger narrative of His redemptive plan.

So, when you find yourself in the midst of a difficult season, take heart. Just as Joseph's trials prepared him for his ultimate purpose, your struggles are not in vain. They are refining your character, strengthening your faith, and equipping you to fulfill the unique call God has placed on your life.

When you experience moments of triumph and blessing,

give thanks. Recognize that these high points are not just for your own enjoyment, but they are part of God's plan to use your story to impact others. As you surrender your life to God daily, trust that He is working all things together for your good and His glory (Romans 8:28). He is the Author and Perfecter of your faith (Hebrews 12:2), and He is writing a beautiful story through your life—a story of redemption, hope, and purpose.

So, embrace your story. Own it, cherish it, and share it with others. Allow God to use your experiences, both the joys and the sorrows, to minister to those around you. Your testimony has the power to bring healing, encouragement, and salvation to countless lives. And as you live out your story, remember that it is not just about you. It is about the God who created you, loves you, and has a plan for your life. It is about the people He has placed in your path, the lives you will touch, and the legacy you will leave.

Your story matters because it is part of God's larger story—a story of love, redemption, and restoration. It is a story that began before the foundation of the world and will continue into eternity. So, don't be afraid to live your story with passion, purpose, and surrender. Trust that God is guiding your every step, and that He will use your unique experiences to accomplish His good purposes.

And as you do, you will discover the joy and fulfillment that comes from living a life fully surrendered to God. You will experience the peace that surpasses understanding, the strength that comes from walking in obedience, and the hope that anchors your soul.

Your story matters, my friend. It matters to God, it

matters to those around you, and it matters to the world. So, live it well. Live it with faith, courage, and surrender. And watch as God uses your story to shape destiny and bring glory to His name.

Your story matters. It's unique, powerful, and can make a difference. Live a story that reflects God's goodness and inspires others.

"For we are God's masterpiece. He has created us anew in Christ Jesus, so we can do the good things he planned for us long ago."
—Ephesians 2:10

132

CHAPTER 19

THE WORK OF THE
HOLY SPIRIT

I N JOHN 14, Jesus is preparing to leave Earth, about to face a sham trial and the cross. His disciples are troubled by this impending separation. If you've ever felt troubled, unsure of what to do, this entry is for you.

Jesus says to His disciples in John 14:1, "Do not let your hearts be troubled. You believe in God; believe also in Me. My Father's house has many rooms; if that were not so, would I have told you that I am going there to prepare a place for you?" Jesus speaks of heaven as a real, tangible place, not a mere figment of our imagination. He assures His disciples, and us, that He is going to prepare a place for us.

Imagine the disciples' anxiety as Jesus tells them He is leaving. They had left everything to follow Him. Their anxiety must have been overwhelming. Jesus continues, "And if I go and prepare a place for you, I will come back and take you to be with Me that you also may be where I am" (vs.3). This promise of Jesus' return is a cornerstone of our hope. It's not just about streets of gold; it's about being with Jesus forever.

In John 14:4, Jesus says, "You know the way to the place where I am going." Thomas, ever the realist, responds, "Lord, we don't know where You are going, so how can we know the way?" Jesus answers, "I am the way and the truth and the life. No one comes to the Father except through Me." The disciples, even after hearing Jesus' words, still felt troubled. They had spent years with Jesus, and now He was leaving.

Many believers acknowledge the Holy Spirit but haven't truly leaned into His presence and power.

Later, in verse 16, Jesus offers a profound promise: "I will ask the Father, and He will give you another advocate to help you and be with you forever—the Spirit of truth." Jesus reassures them that although He is leaving, He will send the Holy Spirit to be with them forever. This Helper, the Holy Spirit, is a crucial yet often overlooked aspect of our faith.

Many believers acknowledge the Holy Spirit but haven't truly leaned into His presence and power. The Holy Spirit is not just a theological concept; He is an active, living presence in our lives. Let's take a closer look at what the Holy Spirit does in our lives.

THE ADVOCATE IN OUR LIVES

The Holy Spirit advocates for us. Jesus says in John 14:16, "I will ask the Father, and He will give you another Helper." The Greek word for "another" used here means, "another of the same kind." Jesus is saying that the Holy Spirit will be just like Him. The term 'Helper' or 'Paraclete' means one who comes alongside to assist. This means that the Holy Spirit stands up for us when we can't stand for ourselves.

As believers, we face an enemy who seeks to undermine our faith and well-being. The enemy, Satan, is described as the accuser who constantly tries to make us doubt our salvation, question our worth, and feel unloved. The Holy Spirit counters these lies by standing as our advocate, reminding us of our identity in Christ and the truth of God's love.

APPLYING TRUTH TO OUR LIVES

The Holy Spirit also applies truth to our lives. In John 14:17, Jesus refers to the Holy Spirit as "the Spirit of truth." The world cannot accept Him because it neither sees Him nor knows Him. But you know Him, for He lives with you and will be in you. The Holy Spirit guides us into all truth, helping us discern right from wrong and illuminating God's Word.

In our day, confusion abounds. The enemy, the father of lies, distorts truth and leads many astray. But the Holy Spirit brings clarity. He helps us understand Scripture, apply its principles to our lives, and discern God's will. This guidance is crucial, especially when we face moral and ethical dilemmas.

BRINGING LEARNING TO LIFE

The Holy Spirit animates our learning. Jesus taught many things during His time on earth, and He promised that the Holy Spirit would help us remember and understand these teachings. In John 14:26, Jesus says, "But the Advocate, the Holy Spirit, whom the Father will send in My name, will teach you all things and will remind you of everything I have said to you."

The Holy Spirit brings the Bible to life, making it relevant to our daily circumstances. He helps us recall scriptures in times of need, providing comfort, guidance, and conviction. This dynamic role of the Holy Spirit ensures that our learning is not just head knowledge but transformative heart knowledge.

ALLEVIATING OUR ANXIETY

In John 14:27, Jesus offers a profound gift: "Peace I leave with you; My peace I give you. I do not give to you as the world gives. Do not let your hearts be troubled and do not be afraid." The Holy Spirit alleviates our anxiety, providing a peace that transcends understanding.

In our fast-paced, stress-filled world, anxiety is rampant. Many of us turn to unhealthy coping mechanisms—substance abuse, overeating, or isolation. But the Holy Spirit offers a better way. He calms our fears, reassures our hearts, and helps us rest in God's promises. His peace is not temporary or superficial; it is deep and abiding.

CONVICTING US OF SIN

Finally, the Holy Spirit convicts us of sin. In John 16:8, Jesus says, "When He comes, He will prove the world to be in the wrong about sin and righteousness and judgment." This conviction is not about condemnation but about transformation. The Holy Spirit reveals areas in our lives that need change, guiding us toward repentance and growth.

This process is like a doctor diagnosing an illness; we need the truth about our condition to receive proper treatment. The Holy Spirit, our divine Physician, shows us our spiritual ailments and helps us find healing and wholeness in Christ.

RESPONDING TO THE HOLY SPIRIT

So, how do we respond to the Holy Spirit's work in our lives? First, we need to recognize the warning signs on the dashboard of our souls. Are we feeling spiritually empty, constantly stressed, or stuck in bad habits? These are indicators that we need to invite the Holy Spirit to do His work in us.

Second, we must ask for His help. In moments of struggle, instead of relying on our strength, we should turn to the Holy Spirit for guidance, comfort, and strength. This could mean pausing to pray, seeking counsel from mature believers, or immersing ourselves in God's Word.

> **Walking in the Spirit requires surrendering our control and letting God lead.**

Finally, we need to trust and obey. Walking in the Spirit requires surrendering our control and letting God lead. It means following His promptings, even when it's uncomfortable or counterintuitive. But as we do, we'll find that His way leads to life, peace, and fulfillment.

Imagine the difference it would make if we truly lived by the Spirit. Instead of feeling like a car without fuel or a ship without wind, we would move forward with purpose and power. We would experience the fullness of life that Jesus promised, resting in His peace, growing in His truth, and shining His light to the world.

Today, let's invite the Holy Spirit to fill our lives afresh. Let's ask Him to advocate for us, apply truth to our hearts, animate our learning, alleviate our anxiety, and convict us of sin. As we do, we'll discover that we are not alone. We have a divine Helper who walks with us, empowering us to live out our faith with joy and confidence.

When life feels uncertain, remember the Holy Spirit is your guide and comforter. Trust in His work in your life, and let your heart be at peace.

"But when the Father sends the Advocate as my representative—that is, the Holy Spirit—he will teach you everything and will remind you of everything I have told you."
—John 14:26

140

CHAPTER 20

DISCOVERING YOUR GOD-GIVEN GIFTS: EMBRACING YOUR UNIQUE PURPOSE

HAVE YOU EVER received a gift and forgotten to put it to use?

My aunt sends a check on every birthday. She determines the amount based on our age: one dollar per year! A few years ago, my wife received her annual check. She appreciated it, but it got tucked away in the card and left in a drawer. As the weeks went by, my aunt called more than once to see if my wife was going to cash the check. Honestly, she had forgotten about the cheque, but after some searching, we finally found it.

I still tease her about it. She could have used the check for new shoes, coffee with friends, or even taking me to dinner! Yet, this freely given gift went untapped. It was a gift wasted. Sometimes, this happens to us, spiritually.

In the tapestry of life, each one of us has been given a unique thread—a spiritual gift that is woven into the very fabric of our being. These gifts, born in the spirit of God, are not mere natural talents or abilities, but rather a super-natural endowment given to every believer for a divine purpose. As we navigate the journey of faith, it is essential that we not only discover these gifts but also learn to embrace and utilize them for the glory of God and the edi-fication of His church.

The Bible tells us in Ephesians 4:7, "But to each one of us grace was given according to the measure of Christ's gift."

Discovering our spiritual gifts is not always a straightforward process, but it is a journey worth embarking on. This powerful truth reminds us that every believer has been graced with a spiritual gift, custom-tailored by the hand of God Himself. These gifts are not reserved for an elite few or those who have reached a certain level of spiritual maturity. Rather, they are freely given to all who have put their faith in Christ, regardless of their background, age, or experience.

So, what exactly are these spiritual gifts, and how do they differ from natural talents? While natural talents are inherent abilities that we possess from birth, spir-itual gifts are supernatural enablements given to us by the Holy Spirit upon our salvation. They are not merely things we are good at, but rather tools that God has entrusted to us, to fulfill His purposes on earth. When we operate in our spiritual gifts, there is a divine fingerprint upon our work—a sense that God Himself is moving through us to accomplish His will.

Discovering our spiritual gifts is not always a straightfor-ward process, but it is a journey worth embarking on. One way to begin is by studying what the Bible says about spiritual gifts in passages, such as 1 Corinthians 12, Romans 12, and 1 Peter 4. As we immerse ourselves in these scriptures, we can ask God to reveal to us the specific gifts He has placed within us. We can also examine our own hearts, paying attention to the things that bring us joy and fulfilment when serving others. Often, our spiritual gifts are closely tied to the passions and burdens that God has laid upon our hearts.

Another helpful tool in discovering our spiritual gifts is to seek the input of others, particularly those who know us well and have seen us in action. Sometimes, the people around us can recognize gifts in us that we may have over-looked or undervalued. Additionally, many churches (like ours) offer spiritual gift assessments or classes that provide insight and guidance in this area.

Once we have identified our spiritual gifts, the next step is to put them into practice. It is not enough to simply know what our gifts are; we must be willing to step out in faith and use them for the benefit of others. This is where the true power of spiritual gifts is unleashed—when they are employed in the context of the body of Christ, the church. As each member of the body uses their unique gifts in harmony with one another, the church is built up, strengthened, and equipped to carry out its mission in the world.

It is important to remember that our spiritual gifts are not given for our own personal gain or glory, but rather for the service of others and the advancement of God's kingdom. When we use our gifts with humility and love, we become conduits of God's grace, allowing Him to work through us in powerful ways. We may not always see the immediate fruit of our labors, but we can trust that God is using our faithfulness to impact lives and bring about His purposes.

As we grow in our understanding and use of our spiritual gifts, we must also be careful not to become overconfident or imbalanced in our approach. Every gift, when taken to an extreme or used in isolation, can have a shadow side. For example, someone with the gift of teaching may become puffed up with knowledge, while someone with the gift of service may burn themselves out by trying to meet every need. It is crucial that we allow our gifts to be tempered by the fruit of the Spirit—love, joy, peace, patience, kindness, goodness, faithfulness, gentleness, and self-control. When our gifts are rooted in a deep, abiding relationship with Christ and exercised with wisdom and discernment, they bring life and blessings to those around us.

Ultimately, the discovery and deployment of our spiritual gifts is not a one-time event, but rather a lifelong journey of growth and obedience. As we walk with Christ and allow His Spirit to work in and through us, our gifts will be refined, sharpened, and multiplied for His glory. May we never lose sight of the incredible privilege and responsibility we have been given as stewards of these divine gifts. Let us eagerly pursue the calling God has placed upon our lives, knowing that as we faithfully use what He has entrusted to us, we are participating in something far greater than ourselves—the building up of His eternal kingdom.

I encourage you to take a step toward discovering or effectively using your gift:

1. **Pray**—Take some time to pray and seek God's direction about your spiritual gifts. Ask Him to reveal the unique ways He has equipped you to serve and make a difference in the world.

2. **Study**—Dive into the scriptures mentioned earlier: 1 Corinthians 12, Romans 12, and 1 Peter v4. Study these passages with an open heart, and let the Holy Spirit speak to you through His Word.

3. **Assess**—Consider taking a spiritual gifts assessment, either online or through your church, to gain further clarity.

4. **Logic Check**—Reach out to trusted friends, family, or mentors who know you well and ask for their insights about the gifts they see in you.

5. **Put Them to Work**—Once you have a better understanding of your gifts, look for opportunities to put them into practice. Volunteer in your church, join a ministry, or start a small group where you can use your gifts to serve others.

Remember, the goal is not only to identify your gifts but to actively use them for God's glory and the benefit of His church. As you step out in faith, be open to learning and growing. Embrace the journey, and trust that God will use your willingness and obedience to make a significant impact.

CHAPTER 21

FINDING YOUR GROOVE AND CREATING A RHYTHM FOR PEACE

DOES LIFE EVER feel out of sync to you? Like you're moving to a mismatched beat, flailing around on the dance floor while everyone else seems to have it all together? Maybe your days are crammed with endless responsibilities, distractions and noise. You have a vague sense of the direction you want to go, but with so many demands and so little margin, that peaceful life you long for remains elusive.

I've been there. We've all been there. And what I've discovered is that peace doesn't happen by accident. You don't just stumble into a life of meaning, purpose and rest. Especially not in a world of relentless busyness and distraction. If we want to live from a place of peace, we need to intentionally create a rhythm for it. We need to build habits and routines that make space for God's presence.

In the Bible, there's a teenage guy named Daniel who

modeled this powerfully. Despite living in a godless culture, getting uprooted from his home, and being pressured to conform at every turn, Daniel stayed rooted. He
remained true to who God made him to be. How did he
do it? I believe Daniel had a 'Rule of Life' long before that
became a buzzword. He had rhythms and routines that
kept him anchored in an unsteady world.

A Rule of Life can sound restrictive, but it's just a trellis—
a support structure that helps us grow in the right direction.
Like a vine needs a trellis to get off the ground and bear fruit,
we need rhythms to help us flourish. Daniel was a young guy
with incredible potential, but that potential was only realized
because his life was oriented around three key things:

First, Daniel's life had a clear direction. When the pagan
king tried to woo him away from his faith, Daniel 1:8 says,
"Daniel made up his mind that he would not defile himself." His life was oriented around knowing God personally,
caring about what God cares about, and honoring God's
power. God's direction guided his decisions. He knew the
target he was aiming for.

I can't hit a target I can't see, and neither can you. Most
of us have a vague sense of where we'd like to end up, but
we lack intentionality. In the busyness, we operate on autopilot. Our lives can feel like we have a hundred browser
tabs open, a bunch of programs running in the background, and everything's moving too fast to fix. We're just
trying to make it through the day.

But what if, instead of being tossed around by competing demands, you were guided by a clear direction? What if instead of striving and straining, you were

propelled by intention and purpose? While the world screams for your attention in a hundred different directions, I believe God is inviting you to orient your whole life around three core areas:

Your being—who you are and who you're becoming

Your doing—what you do with your time and talents

Your relating—how you love and connect with others

Here's the thing: You don't have to tackle every area of your life right away. Don't overcomplicate this. Keep it simple and start by listening to God's voice, picking one or two areas to focus on. Where do you sense him calling you to grow? What direction does he want to take you? Set a course and steady your ship.

Secondly, Daniel's direction was refined by his decisions. The destination in his head determined his action steps. When he was pressured to compromise, Daniel resolved to put God first, get input from wise friends, and obey no matter what it cost him. Consistent, daily choices kept him true to his overall direction.

What daily decisions will keep you pointing true North? Maybe it's creating intentional space to connect with God, or reaching out to encourage your spouse, or scheduling time to recharge doing something life-giving. Small, consistent investments in the right direction will take you to incredible places over time. You don't need a sweeping overhaul all at once. Just take the next right step.

And that leads to the last component: demonstration. Daniel's direction and decisions led to a powerful display of God's faithfulness. His seemingly small acts of obedience added up to a lifetime of incredible impact. Daniel had personal victories, professional success, and a platform to influence kings and kingdoms. But more than that, his life is still bearing fruit today. Generations later, we're still talking about this teenage guy who had the resolve to live with uncompromising integrity.

That's the power of living from a place of peace and purpose. When you take the long view, today's decisions take on greater significance. How you live today has a ripple effect. Sure, you might be able to overpower your way to accomplishing great things in a day. But a lifetime of steady faithfulness? That's rare. And powerful.

As you find your groove and create space for God's peace, trust that He will establish your steps.

Imagine, decades from now, your kids and grandkids are visiting the place where you're buried. What would you want them to say about you? My guess is, they won't be talking about your busyness or your professional accolades. They'll be remembering and honoring the huge impact you had on their lives and the way you made time to really see them. They'll reminisce about your unwavering faith that anchored you and the peace you carried into every room.

That's the trajectory I want to set my life on. I don't want the rat race; I want the rhythm. I want to live each day in light of eternity. I want to look up from the daily grind and be crystal clear on where I'm going and why it matters.

As you find your groove and create space for God's peace, trust that He will establish your steps. He will guide and provide in ways that blow your mind. Moment by moment, decision by decision, he'll lead you in a direction more wonderful than you ever thought possible.

So, take heart and be encouraged. Fix your eyes on the one who can take your fragmented days and weave them into a compelling story—a story not just of success, but of significance. A story not of striving, but of abiding.

May you walk in the unforced rhythms of grace and may the peace of God guard your heart as you go.

CHAPTER 22

WHO ARE YOU BECOMING?

TEN YEARS FROM now, who do you want to be? What kind of life do you envision for yourself? More joy, stronger relationships, a deeper faith? Or just more of the same?

The truth is that the person you'll be a decade from now will be determined by the habits you cultivate today. Sounds simple, right? But then why do so many of us struggle to make lasting change?

As humans, we tend to overestimate what we can do in a day and underestimate what we can accomplish through small, consistent actions over time. We set lofty New Year's resolutions, only to abandon them a few weeks later. We mistake intention for action and wonder why our lives aren't changing.

The Apostle Paul understood this struggle. In his letter to the Galatians, he outlines four principles that, when applied, have the power to radically transform our lives:

1. The Principle of Sowing: You reap what you sow.

Whatever you plant, that's what you'll harvest. If you sow seeds of spiritual discipline, you'll reap a rich spiritual life. If you sow seeds of self-destruction, you'll reap a life of chaos and pain. The choice is yours.

2. The Principle of Seasons: You reap more than you sow.

Just as a single seed can produce a bountiful crop, our habits compound over time, leading to exponential growth—for better or for worse. Small, smart choices lived out consistently will take you to places you never thought possible.

3. The Principle of Success: You reap later than you sow.

We live in a culture of instant gratification, but lasting change takes time. Just as a farmer must wait patiently for their crop to mature, we must trust the process and keep showing up, even when we don't see immediate results. Success is a journey, not a destination.

4. The Principle of the Start: Your actions are stronger than your intentions.

The best time to plant a tree was 20 years ago. The second-best time is now. If you want to see change in your life, you can't just think about it or talk about it, you have to actually do something. And there's no better time to start than today.

So, what seeds are you planting in your life right now? Are they seeds of intentionality, faith, and growth? Or are you sowing seeds of procrastination, doubt, and stagnation?

If you're not happy with the harvest you're reaping, it's time to get honest about what you're planting. And that starts with getting clear on who you want to become.

Imagine meeting the future version of yourself. What would they be proud of? What habits and rhythms would they be grateful you started today? Maybe it's a daily practice of prayer and Scripture reading. Maybe it's consistently investing in your most important relationships. Maybe it's finally pursuing that God-given dream that's been tugging at your heart.

Whatever it is, don't wait for someday. Start small but start now. Choose to train, not just try. Embrace the process, trust the journey, and watch as God transforms your life from the inside out. And remember, you're not in this alone. As you seek to cultivate a life of purpose and peace, know that your Heavenly Father is with you every step of the way. He's the Master Gardener, tenderly nurturing the seeds you plant and bringing forth a harvest beyond your wildest dreams.

> **Embrace the process, trust the journey, and watch as God transforms your life from the inside out.**

So, take heart, my friend. The habits you build today will shape the person you become tomorrow. And with God's grace and your intentional action, that future self will be one who radiates joy, peace, and purpose—a living testament to the transformative power of small seeds planted in faith.

Remember, lasting change is possible. You have what it takes. And most importantly, you have a God who is for you, with you, and working through you to bring about His good purposes. So, plant those seeds, tend them faithfully, and trust that in due time, you will reap a harvest of righteousness, peace, and joy that will transform not only your own life but the lives of those around you.

Here's to becoming the person God created you to be, one small, faithful step at a time.

The person you'll be in ten years is shaped by the habits you build today. Start small, stay consistent, and let God guide your transformation.

"And I am certain that God, who began the good work within you, will continue his work until it is finally finished on the day when Christ Jesus returns."
—PHILIPPIANS 1:6

CHAPTER 23

ANCHORED: HOW TO STOP DRIFTING AND START LIVING WITH PURPOSE

AVE YOU EVER felt like you're just drifting through life, carried along by the currents of busyness, distraction, and doubt? You had good intentions at the start of the year—to grow closer to God, to invest in your relationships, to become the person He created you to be. But somewhere along the way, you lost your sense of direction. You find yourself wondering, "How did I end up here?"

If that resonates with you, you're not alone. As humans, we are prone to wander and prone to drift. But here's the good news: we don't have to stay adrift. God has given us anchors to keep us tethered to His truth, His presence, and His purposes for our lives.

In the book of Hebrews, the writer uses a powerful metaphor to describe the hope we have in Jesus. He says, "We have this hope as an anchor for the soul, firm and secure" (Hebrews 6:19). Just as an anchor keeps a ship from drifting aimlessly in the wind and waves, Jesus is the anchor that keeps us grounded in a chaotic world. But what does it look like to drop anchor and live a life of purpose and peace?

I believe there are three key principles we can learn from this passage:

1. Decide on a fixed direction.

If you've ever been boating, you know that the first step to getting where you want to go is to chart your course. You must know your destination and the direction you need to head to get there. The same is true in life. We can't just drift along and expect to end up somewhere meaningful. We must intentionally set our sights on the right target.

For followers of Jesus, that target is knowing Him and making Him known. It's living in a way that reflects His character and advances His kingdom. When we fix our eyes on Jesus, the author and perfecter of our faith (Hebrews 12:2), everything else falls into place. Our priorities, our decisions, our relationships—they all align with His purposes.

But here's the thing: deciding on a direction is a daily choice. We must continually reorient ourselves to true north, because the currents of culture and the distractions of life are constantly trying to pull us off-course. That's why we need the next principle...

2. Develop foundational disciplines.

Disciplines are the habits and practices that keep us tethered to truth. They are the spiritual muscles we exercise to grow in godliness and stay on track with God's plan for our lives.

For me, three foundational disciplines have been essential: engaging with the gospel, reading God's Word, and being part of God's church. When I regularly remind myself of the good news that Jesus died for my sins and rose again to give me new life, it recalibrates my heart. When I spend time in Scripture, it renews my mind and shapes my perspective. And when I do life with other believers in the context of church community, it sharpens and encourages me in ways I couldn't experience on my own.

Disciplines aren't always easy or convenient. They require intentionality and commitment. But over time, as we consistently practice them, they produce a harvest of righteousness and peace in our lives (Hebrews 12:11). They keep us anchored when the storms of life threaten to sweep us away.

3. Demonstrate faithful devotion.

Dropping anchor is not a one-time event; it's a lifestyle of faithfulness. It's showing up day after day, season after season, and saying, "Jesus, I'm Yours. I'm all in."

Faithfulness is not flashy. It doesn't usually make headlines or go viral on social media. But it's the stuff that real, lasting impact is made of. It's the cumulative effect of a thousand small choices to trust God, obey His Word, and love others well.

When we demonstrate faithful devotion over the long haul, something powerful happens: our lives begin to bear fruit; we experience a deeper sense of God's presence and purpose. We have opportunities to shine His light in dark places. We leave a legacy that points people to Jesus.

Faithfulness is not about perfection; it's about persistence.

It's getting back up when we stumble, repenting when we sin, and pressing on toward the goal (Philippians 3:14). It's believing that God is faithful even when we are faithless (2 Timothy 2:13), and that He who began a good work in us will carry it on to completion (Philippians 1:6).

So, if you find yourself drifting today, take heart. The anchor still holds. Jesus is still the firm foundation, the solid rock on which we can build our lives (Matthew 7:24–25). His grace is still sufficient, His power is still made perfect in our weakness (2 Corinthians 12:9).

It won't always be easy, but it will always be worth it.

What do you need to do to drop anchor today? What direction do you need to decide on? What disciplines do you need to develop? How can you demonstrate faithful devotion in the dailiness of life?

Don't let the currents of culture or the distractions of the enemy keep you from the abundant life Jesus came to give you (John 10:10). Fix your eyes on Him, lock arms with His people, and set sail on the adventure He has for you. It won't always be easy, but it will always be worth it.

As the old hymn says, "We have an anchor that keeps the soul / Steadfast and sure while the billows roll / Fastened to the Rock move / Grounded firm and deep in the Savior's love"(P.J. Owens, 1882). May this be true of you and me today, and every day forward.

If you feel like you're drifting through life, it's time to anchor yourself in God's purpose. Don't let distractions steer you off course—live intentionally for Him.

"Therefore, we who have fled to him for refuge can have great confidence as we hold to the hope that lies before us. This hope is a strong and trustworthy anchor for our souls."
—HEBREWS 6:18-19

164

CHAPTER 24

THE WAITING ROOM: WHERE FAITH MEETS DOUBT

HAVE YOU EVER felt like your life is one big waiting room? You're stuck in this space between where you are and where you desperately want to be. Maybe you're waiting for healing, for a relationship to be restored, for a breakthrough in your career, or for a long-held dream to finally come true. And with each passing day, the wait feels harder, the doubts grow louder, and the questions get bigger.

If that's you, I want you to know you're not alone. In fact, you're in good company. Throughout Scripture, we see stories of people who had to wait on God—people like Abraham, Joseph, David, and Paul. But today, I want to focus on someone who often gets overlooked: John the Baptist.

John was a man on a mission. From birth, he was set apart to prepare the way for the promised Messiah. He spent his life preaching one message: "Repent, for the kingdom of heaven is at hand!" (Matthew 3:2). And when Jesus showed up on the scene, John was the first to recognize him. "Behold, the Lamb of God, who takes away the sin of the world!" he declared (John 1:29).

But then, in a shocking twist, this bold prophet ends up in prison. Locked away in a cell, facing execution, John starts to doubt. "Are you the one who is to come, or shall we look for another?" he asks Jesus (Matthew 11:3).

Wait, what? This is the same John who baptized Jesus, who saw the Spirit descend on him like a dove, who heard the Father's voice from heaven saying, "This is my beloved Son, with whom I am well pleased" (Matthew 3:17). How could he question if Jesus was really the Messiah? The answer is simple: John was human. And like all of us, his faith was not immune to the weight of waiting.

When we're stuck in the waiting room, our problems seem bigger, our doubts seem louder, and our faith seems smaller.

You see, waiting has a way of warping our perspective. When we're stuck in the waiting room, our problems seem bigger, our doubts seem louder, and our faith seems smaller. We start to wonder if God is, in fact, good and we doubt if he really cares, or if he actually has a plan.

But here's the thing: our feelings are not always reliable indicators of reality. Just because we feel forgotten doesn't mean we are. Just because we feel abandoned doesn't mean we've been. Just because we can't see God working doesn't mean he's not. That's why we need a theology of waiting—a framework for understanding God's character and purposes even when our circumstances are confusing and painful. And that's exactly what Jesus gives John in his response.

"Go and tell John what you hear and see," Jesus says.

> *The blind receive their sight and the lame walk, lepers are cleansed and the deaf hear, and the dead are raised up, and the poor have good news preached to them. And blessed is the one who is not offended by me (Matthew 11:4-6).*

In other words, Jesus is saying something like, "John, I know you're struggling. I know you're doubting. But don't let your circumstances blind you to the truth of who I am and what I'm doing. The kingdom is breaking through, even if it doesn't look like what you expected."

And that is the heart of a theology of waiting. It's the stubborn belief that God is still good, still sovereign, and still at work, even when the evidence seems slim. It's the decision to cling to what we know rather than what we feel. It's the willingness to trust that our waiting is not wasted, that God is using even the delays and disappointments to shape us into the people he created us to be.

I'll be honest: embracing this theology is not easy. There have been times in my own life when the wait felt unbearable, when the doubts felt overpowering, and when the darkness felt suffocating. I've had moments, like John, when I've wondered if God is really who He says he is, if his promises are true, and if His plan is really good.

But in those moments, I've had to make a choice. I've had to choose to anchor my soul in what I know rather than what I feel. I've had to choose to fix my eyes on Jesus, the author and perfecter of my faith (Hebrews 12:2). I've had to choose to believe that my waiting is not wasted, that God is using even the hardest parts of my story to write a narrative of redemption and hope. And slowly, painfully, miraculously, I've seen him do just that. I've seen him bring beauty from ashes, strength from weakness, and joy from sorrow. I've seen him use my waiting to deepen my faith, to teach me empathy, to make me more like Jesus.

So, if you find yourself in the waiting room today, can I just encourage you? Don't give up, don't lose heart, and don't let your doubts drown out the voice of truth. Keep showing up, keep reaching out, keep holding on to Jesus. He hasn't forgotten you and he hasn't abandoned you. He sees you; he knows you, and he loves you with an ever-lasting love. He is using your waiting to accomplish purposes you may not be able to see or understand yet.

Cling to his promises and lean into his presence. Trust in his timing and know that one day, the waiting will be over. One day, every tear will be wiped away, every question will be answered, and every longing will be fulfilled. But until then, may you find comfort in the truth that you are not alone. May you find strength in the God who holds you in the palm of his hand. May you find hope in the Savior who endured the ultimate waiting on the cross, and who now lives to intercede for you.

May your waiting room become a sacred space, a place where your faith is refined, your character is shaped, and your dependence on God is deepened. May it be a place where you learn to say with confidence, "I trust you, Jesus.

I believe you're still good, still sovereign, and still at work. And I will wait for you as long as it takes."

He is worth the wait. And he will meet you in the waiting with grace, with peace, and with the power to persevere. Keep holding on and keep believing. Keep fixing your eyes on the one who is faithful, now and forevermore.

170

CHAPTER 25

EVEN NOW

I'VE NEVER BEEN good at waiting. I'm the guy who refreshes his email inbox every 30 seconds when expecting an important message. I'm the one who paces anxiously in front of the microwave, willing it to heat my leftovers faster. Patience has never been my strong suit.

But lately, I've been thinking a lot about waiting. Not the mundane kind of waiting we do in grocery store lines or doctor's offices. I'm talking about the deep, soul-wrenching kind of waiting. The kind where you're desperately hoping for something—praying for it with everything you've got—but the answer just doesn't seem to come.

Maybe you know the feeling. You've been praying for years to conceive a child, watching others around you get pregnant at the drop of a hat. Or perhaps you're waiting for that prodigal son or daughter to come back to faith after wandering far from God. Perhaps you're stuck in a dead-end job, sending out resume after resume, waiting for a career breakthrough that feels impossibly far away.

Whatever it is, this kind of waiting can wear on your soul. It's easy to get discouraged, to wonder if God is even listening. You question if He cares at all about our struggles and longings.

I was reminded of this recently when reading the story of Lazarus in John 11. It's a familiar tale: Jesus' friend Lazarus falls ill, and his sisters, Mary and Martha, send word hoping Jesus will come heal him. But Jesus delays, and by the time He arrives, Lazarus has been dead for four days.

I've read this story dozens of times, but the last time I read it, something struck me differently. I realized how easy it is to gloss over the raw emotions Mary and Martha must have felt in those agonizing days of waiting.

These weren't casual acquaintances of Jesus; they were his close friends. The text says Jesus loved them deeply. So, when they sent word that Lazarus was sick, they likely expected Jesus to drop everything and rush to his side. I can imagine their growing anxiety and confusion as the hours and days ticked by with no word from Jesus.

"Surely, He'll come soon," they may have reassured each other on the first day of waiting. By the second day, doubt probably started to creep in. "What's taking Him so long? Doesn't He care that Lazarus is dying?" On the third day, hope may have given way to anger and hurt. "How could He abandon us like this? We thought we were His friends!"

By the fourth day, with Lazarus' body already in the tomb, I imagine they felt betrayed and hopeless. Their belief in Jesus' power and love had been shaken to the core.

When Jesus finally arrives, Martha's pain and confusion are evident. "Lord, if you had been here, my brother would not have died," she says, a mixture of faith and frustration in her voice.

I relate to Martha in that moment. How many times have I prayed desperately for God to show up, only to be met with silence? How often have I cried out, "Lord, where are you? Why aren't you answering?"

In those times of waiting, it's so easy for doubt to creep in and to wonder if God really cares or if He's even listening at all. Our faith can start to waver and wane. But here's the thing that struck me as I pondered this story: Jesus had a plan all along. His delay wasn't due to indifference or neglect. He was orchestrating something far greater than Mary and Martha could have imagined.

The hard part is, we can't see the end of the story while we're in the middle of it.

They wanted Jesus to heal their sick brother. But Jesus wanted to raise their dead brother to life. They were hoping for a doctor, but Jesus came as the resurrection and the life itself. Their prayers were good, but God's plans were better. His answer exceeded their wildest expectations.

I wonder how often that's true in our own lives? We pray for the sick person to be made well, when God wants to bring the dead to life. We ask for small improvements, when God is working on total transformation.

The hard part is, we can't see the end of the story while we're in the middle of it. Mary and Martha didn't have John 11 to read, so they couldn't flip ahead a few pages to see that their pain would turn to indescribable joy. All they knew in that moment was grief, confusion, and a sense that Jesus had let them down.

I think that's where many of us find ourselves in seasons of waiting. We can't see how our story ends, and we don't know what God is up to behind the scenes. And so, we're faced with a choice: will we trust Him even when we can't trace Him?

It's not an easy choice. Trusting God in the waiting doesn't mean we don't feel pain or frustration. It doesn't mean plastering on a fake smile and pretending everything is fine. Martha was honest about her hurt and confusion, even as she clung to faith that Jesus could still do something.

"But even now I know that whatever you ask from God, God will give you," she tells Jesus.

Even now, after days of silence, and after her brother's death. Even in her grief and pain, Martha chooses to believe that Jesus is still good, still powerful, still worthy of her trust.

I love the phrase, "even now." It's an anthem of stubborn hope in the face of disappointment. A declaration that our circumstances don't define God's character or limit His power.

Even now, when the diagnosis is grim.

Even now, when the relationship seems beyond repair.

Even now, when the dream feels dead and buried.

We can still trust that God is working. Still believe that He hears our cries. Still hope that He can bring beauty from ashes and life from death. Easier said than done, I know. So, how do we cultivate that kind of resilient faith? How do we keep hoping when we're tempted to give up?

I think it starts with being honest—with ourselves and with God. It's okay to tell God we're hurting, confused, even angry. He can handle our raw emotions. In fact, I believe He welcomes that kind of authentic conversation more than our polite, sanitized prayers.

We also need community around us in seasons of waiting. People who will weep with us, remind us of God's faithfulness, and hold onto hope on our behalf when we're struggling to believe. I'm grateful for friends who have done that for me in dark seasons.

Most importantly, we need to continually realign our hearts with truth. Our feelings are valid, but they're not always trustworthy guides. That's why we need to regularly immerse ourselves in Scripture, reminding ourselves of who God is and what He's promised.

The Psalms are especially helpful here. They give voice to the full range of human emotion —joy and sorrow, faith and doubt, praise and lament. They show us it's possible to be brutally honest with God while still trusting in His goodness.

I love how Psalm 13 begins with raw anguish, "How long, O Lord? Will you forget me forever?" but ends with a choice to trust: "But I have trusted in your steadfast love; my heart shall rejoice in your salvation."

This is the kind of resilient faith I want. Not a faith that denies pain or plasters on a fake smile, but a faith that can look suffering in the face and still declare, "Yet I will hope in God."

It's not easy and some days it feels impossible, but I'm learning that great disappointments can become fertile ground for great miracles. The seasons of waiting, as painful as they are, can deepen our faith in beautiful ways if we let them.

I'm reminded of a quote I once heard: "If it hasn't worked out yet, then it's not the end." I love that perspective. It reminds me that God isn't finished writing my story—or yours. Even in our darkest moments, He is still at work behind the scenes.

So, if you find yourself in a season of waiting today, take heart. Your cries haven't fallen on deaf ears. Your tears haven't gone unnoticed. The God who wept at Lazarus' tomb weeps with you in your pain. But He also calls you to hope. To trust that even now—especially now - He is able to do immeasurably more than all we ask or imagine.

Let's allow truth to drive us back to trust and to invite Christ into the middle of our crisis.

Maybe, like Mary and Martha, you'll discover that God's "no" or "not yet" was only to set the stage for a greater "yes" than you could have dreamed. Perhaps your season of waiting is preparing you for a miracle beyond your wildest hopes.

Or maybe your prayer won't be answered in the way you're longing for. Maybe God has a different plan, one you can't see or understand right now. Even then, we can trust that He is good, that He loves us, that He is working all things for our ultimate good and His glory.

Let's choose to keep believing, even when we can't see, to keep serving, even when we don't feel like it and to keep asking, even when the answer seems delayed. Let's allow truth to drive us back to trust and to invite Christ into the middle of our crisis. Let's allow the "even now" moments where we declare our faith in God's goodness, even as we honestly express our pain. And let's remember that we're not alone in the waiting. The God who is the resurrection and the life Himself walks with us, He feels our pain, He bottles our tears, and He promises that one day, all our waiting will give way to wonder as we see the fullness of His plan unveiled.

Until then, may we learn to wait well, to trust deeply, and to hope stubbornly in the God who is able to do far more abundantly than all we ask or think.

Even now. Especially now.

CHAPTER 26

CROSSING YOUR JORDAN

HAVE YOU EVER felt stuck? Like there's this insurmountable obstacle between you and where God wants you to be? Maybe it's a relationship that seems beyond repair, an addiction you can't shake, or a dream that feels impossibly out of reach. If so, you're in good company. The people of Israel faced their own seemingly impassable barrier: the Jordan River.

Picture this: After 40 years of wandering in the desert, the Israelites are finally on the cusp of entering the Promised Land. But between them and their destiny lies the Jordan River. It's not the gentle stream you might imagine, but a raging torrent one mile wide, flowing at 40 miles per hour. It's flood season, and the usual fords are submerged. How are they going to cross this?

This story from Joshua 3 isn't just ancient history; It's a picture of our own spiritual journeys. We all have 'Jordans' in our lives—obstacles that seem too big and too daunting to overcome. But here's the good news: where we see no way, God is in the business of building highways.

So, how do we get from being stuck to celebrating? How do we cross our personal Jordans and step into all that God has for us? The story of Israel's crossing gives us a powerful three-step process:

1. Chase After the Move of God

The first step is simple, but crucial: we need to get our eyes on God. For the Israelites, this meant literally fixing their gaze on the Ark of the Covenant, the physical representation of God's presence among them. Joshua instructed the people to follow the Ark when it moved, staying about half a mile behind it so everyone could see.

What does this look like for us today? It means intentionally seeking God's presence and activity in our lives. It means tuning our hearts to recognize where He's already at work and joining Him there.

Too often, we try to forge ahead in our own strength, asking God to bless our plans. But real transformation happens when we align ourselves with what God is already doing. It's not about us doing great things for God, but about God doing great things through us as we faithfully follow Him.

This requires a shift in perspective. Instead of asking, "God, where are you in my mess?", we need to start asking, "God, where are you moving, and how can I join you?" It's about developing spiritual eyesight to see God's hand at work, even in unlikely places.

Remember, Jesus didn't come just to keep you out of your mess, but to walk through your mess with you. He's not waiting for you on the other side of the Jordan; He's right there with you, ready to make a way where there seems to be no way.

2. Prepare for the Journey

The second step is all about heart preparation. Joshua told the people to "consecrate" or purify themselves because the next day, God was going to do wonders among them (Joshua 3:5). This wasn't just about external cleanliness; it was about getting their hearts ready to witness and participate in God's miraculous work.

For us, this preparation starts with dealing with our sin. Ouch, right? Nobody likes to talk about sin these days. It's much more comfortable to focus on God's love and acceptance. God's love and acceptance are absolutely true and vital, but if we want to experience the fullness of what God has for us, we need to be honest about the things in our lives that are holding us back.

> The beautiful thing is, when we bring our mess to Jesus, He doesn't condemn us, He embraces us.

This isn't about beating yourself up or wallowing in guilt. It's about bringing everything—the good, the bad, and the ugly—into the light of God's love. It's about saying, "God, here's my anger, my pride, my addiction, my fear. I can't handle these on my own. I need your forgiveness and your power to change."

The beautiful thing is, when we bring our mess to Jesus, He doesn't condemn us, He embraces us. He says, "Let me have it, give me a hug. Come on, let's go and do that one again." His love is big enough to handle all our junk.

Preparing our hearts also means putting on our 'spiritual glasses,' which means cultivating an attitude of expectancy and awareness. Mother Teresa put it beautifully, "I will set aside the typical and put my Spirit on alert to see where God is working around me, so that I can join him."

This might look like starting your day with a simple prayer: "God, I want to hear from you today. Give me direction, purpose, and wisdom. I want to see you at work. Amen." It's about training ourselves to look for God's fingerprints in our everyday lives.

3. Step Out and Stand Still

This final step might seem contradictory, but it's where the rubber meets the road in our faith journey. There comes a point where we need to take action—to step out in faith—and then learn to be still and trust God to do what only He can do.

For the Israelites, this meant the priests carrying the Ark had to step into the raging Jordan before the waters parted. Can you imagine how terrifying that must have been? But as soon as their feet touched the water, the flow stopped upstream, and the river stood up like a wall.

In our lives, this might look like taking that first step towards reconciliation in a broken relationship, or finally seeking help for an addiction, or stepping out to pursue that God-given dream. It's about moving forward in faith, even when we can't see the whole path ahead.

But here's the key: after we step out, we need to learn to stand still and depend fully on God. Too often, we try to muscle our way through our problems in our own strength. But some Jordans are too big for us to cross alone, and we need to reach the end of ourselves and learn to rely completely on God's power.

This is where real transformation happens. When we fully surrender, the world might call us fools, but Jesus says to wear it like a badge of honor because He's going to carry us through.

Remember, faith moves us forward in God's way and in God's timing, and God's timing is rarely on our schedule! He's a most inconvenient God. If He operated on our time-table, He wouldn't be God, we would be. God doesn't fit into our wristwatch; He fits us into His universe. And in His perfect timing, He calls us to join Him in His work.

BUILDING YOUR MEMORIAL

After the Israelites crossed the Jordan, God instructed them to take stones from the riverbed and build a memorial. This wasn't just a history lesson; it was a visual reminder of God's faithfulness for generations to come.

We need these kinds of reminders in our lives, too. It's so easy to forget what God has done for us, especially when we face new challenges. That's why it can be powerful to create tangible reminders of God's work in our lives.

Maybe for you, that's journaling about answered prayers. Maybe it's creating a piece of art that represents a break-through God gave you. Or maybe, like the church in this message, you write a word or phrase on a rock to keep somewhere visible.

The point isn't the specific method; it's about training yourself to remember and celebrate God's faithfulness. It's about building a history with God that you can look back on when you face new Jordans in our lives.

YOUR NEXT STEP

So, where are you in this journey? Are you staring at your Jordan, wondering how you'll ever cross it? Are you stuck on the banks, too afraid to step into the water? Or are you in the middle of the river, waiting for God to part the waters?

Wherever you are, know this: the God who parted the Jordan is the same God who is with you today. He specializes in making a way where there seems to be no way.

Remember, nothing is too difficult for the God of all creation. He can do immeasurably more than all we ask or imagine. So, fix your eyes on Jesus, prepare your heart to follow Him, and be ready to move when He calls.

Your Jordan might look impossible today but with God, impossibility is just His starting point for a miracle. Trust Him, follow Him, and get ready to see Him make a way where there seems to be no way.

Let's cross this Jordan together. The Promised Land is waiting on the other side.

When you face an obstacle that seems impossible to cross, remember God's power is greater. Step out in faith, and watch Him make a way.

"When you go through deep waters, I will be with you. When you go through rivers of difficulty, you will not drown."
—Isaiah 43:2

CHAPTER 27

WHERE DO WE GO FROM HERE?

A s FOLLOWERS OF Jesus, we all want to live a life that works—a life that makes a difference, a life that honors God, a life filled with purpose and meaning. But what does that look like in practice? Is there an example we can follow?

In the book of Philippians, the apostle Paul points us to the ultimate example of a life that works: the life of Jesus Christ himself. By examining Jesus' attitude and actions, we discover the keys to living out our faith in a way that is compelling and transformative.

Let's explore three crucial questions that flow from Philippians 2 and Jesus' example:

Question 1: What Does God Want? (Philippians 2:5-8)

The first key to a life that works is having the same attitude as Christ Jesus. Though he was fully God, Jesus did not cling to his divine privileges. Instead, he willingly emptied himself, humbled himself, and became a servant. He was obedient to the Father's will, even to the point of dying a criminal's death on the cross.

This radical humility and obedience characterized Jesus' entire earthly ministry. At his baptism, at the start of his public ministry, the Father's affirming voice declared, "This is my beloved Son, with whom I am well pleased" (Matthew 3:17). Jesus was all about doing the Father's will.

Later, when tempted in the wilderness, Jesus responded to each of Satan's enticements not by asserting his own desires or flexing his divine power, but by quoting Scripture, aligning himself with God's purposes (Matthew 4:1–11). Even in Gethsemane, as he contemplated the agony of the cross, Jesus prayed, "Nevertheless, not as I will, but as you will" (Matthew 26:39).

Throughout his life, Jesus' consuming passion was to do the will of his Father. As his followers, we are called to adopt that same posture. Rather than being driven by selfish ambition or conceit, we must humbly seek God's agenda above our own.

Throughout his life, Jesus' consuming passion was to do the will of his Father.

What would it look like to approach each area of life with the question, "God, what do you want?" What if we asked that of our physical health, our relationships, our finances, our thoughts, our families, our work, our spiritual growth, our community engagement, even our recreation?

Adopting a "what does God want?" mindset realigns our priorities. It also shifts our focus from self to God. Like Jesus, we find joy not in fulfilling our own agendas but in humbly embracing the Father's good, pleasing, and perfect will (Romans 12:2).

Question 2: Who Can I Serve? (Philippians 2:3–4)

Knowing what God wants is essential, but it's incomplete without action. The rubber meets the road in service. Once again, Jesus models the way.

"Do nothing from selfish ambition or conceit," Paul writes, "but in humility count others more significant than yourselves. Let each of you look not only to his own interests, but also to the interests of others" (vv. 3–4). In other words, following Jesus means living beyond ourselves; it means valuing others above ourselves and actively seeking to meet their needs.

Jesus certainly lived this out. He noticed the hungry and fed them, not just physically but spiritually (Mark 6:34–44). He crossed social boundaries to engage the hurting and marginalized, like the Samaritan woman at the well (John 4). He stopped to heal the sick, even when it was inconvenient or controversial (Mark 1:40–45; 3:1–6). He washed his disciples' dirty feet, taking the posture of the lowliest servant and calling them to do the same (John 13:1–17).

For us today, a life that works is marked by incarnational service. It's rolling up our sleeves and asking, "Who can I serve? Who is God calling me to value, to love, to pour into?" Maybe it's the elderly neighbor who could use a helping hand or a listening ear. Maybe it's the coworker who seems discouraged and could use a word of encouragement. Maybe it's the child who needs a mentor, someone to look up to and learn from.

Service is where discipleship gets practical. It's where love is made visible and tangible. And it's not just for the super-spiritual or unusually gifted. Every Christian, regardless of age or stage, has a part to play. Even students and young people can make an eternal difference by finding ways to serve in their schools, their church, and their community.

The question is, are we willing to set aside our egos, our comfort, our self-interest for the sake of others? Will we dare to live as Jesus did, pouring ourselves out in humble service? That's where joy is found. That's a life that works.

Question 3: Am I Prepared for Eternity? (Philippians 2:9-11)

As important as humble obedience and sacrificial service are, they only make sense in light of eternity. Jesus' earthly life cannot be divorced from his heavenly exaltation. His incarnation and His cross were all means to an end—bringing glory to God and bringing many sons and daughters to glory (Hebrews 2:10).

Paul makes this clear. Because of Jesus' obedience, because of his humility,

> God has highly exalted him and bestowed on him the name that is above every name, so that at the name of Jesus every knee should bow, in heaven and on earth and under the earth, and every tongue confess that Jesus Christ is Lord, to the glory of God the Father (vv. 9-11).

One day, all of creation will bow before King Jesus. All wrongs will be made right, all hidden things brought to light. Those who are in Christ will rejoice, finally seeing their Savior face to face. But those who have rejected him will realize, too late, the horrible mistake they've made.

So, we must ask: Am I prepared for that day? Is my life

oriented around the reality of eternity? Am I investing in things that will last? Am I leveraging my time, my talents, and my relationships to bring as many people as possible into right relationship with God?

That's the clarity Jesus lived with. He endured the agony of the cross "for the joy that was set before him" (Hebrews 12:2)—the joy of bringing glory to the Father, the joy of ushering men and women into eternal life—and he calls us to live with that same eternal perspective.

A life that works is a life anchored in Jesus Christ. It's a life that asks, "God, what do you want?" and realigns every priority around his desires. It's a life spent in whole-hearted, humble service, pouring ourselves out for the good of others. And it's a life laser-focused on eternity, leveraging every moment to bring God glory and point people to Jesus.

This is the life Jesus pioneered for us. It won't always be easy, and it will involve hard choices, sacrifices, and set-backs. But it's the path to true, enduring joy and satisfaction. It's the life we were made for.

As we endeavor to walk in Christ's footsteps, let's encourage one another. Let's spur one another on to love and do good works (Hebrews 10:24). And let's never lose sight of the prize, the upward call of God in Christ Jesus.

One day, every knee will bow, and every tongue will confess that he is Lord. On that day, may we hear those precious words, "Well done, good and faithful servant." May our lives work for His glory.

CLOSING

DEAR FRIEND,

As we come to the close of this journey together, we want to leave you with a few final thoughts.

First, we hope this book has reaffirmed for you that your story matters. You are not here by accident; God created you on purpose, for a purpose. He has a unique plan and calling for your life. No matter what challenges or setbacks you face, remember that in Christ, you have everything you need to live out that calling. In Him, you are more than a conqueror.

Second, we pray that these pages have reminded you of the power of small steps in the right direction. Growing in our relationship with God is not about perfection, but persistence. It's showing up day after day, moment by moment, and choosing to trust and obey, even when we don't feel like it. Those seemingly insignificant acts of faithfulness add up over time to a life transformed by grace. So, keep moving forward, one step at a time.

Finally, as you go from here, cling to Jesus. He is the vine, and apart from Him we can do nothing. But as we abide in Him, as we stay rooted in His Word and connected to His Body, He promises to produce much fruit in us and through us. When the storms come, and they will come, anchor your soul in the unshakable hope of the gospel. Let it be your firm foundation.

My friend, God is not finished with you yet. The best is yet to come. He who began a good work in you will bring it to completion. And one day, when you see Him face to face, it will all be worth it. Every struggle, every sacrifice, every act of obedience—it will pale in comparison to the surpassing worth of knowing Christ Jesus our Lord.

So, fix your eyes on Him and fight the good fight of faith. Keep pursuing the upward call of God in Christ Jesus. He is able to do immeasurably more than we can ask or imagine, and He is with you always, even to the end of the age.

It's been a joy to share this journey with you. May you continue to grow in your faith and may your life shine brightly for His glory.

Many Blessings,
Chuck and Bobby

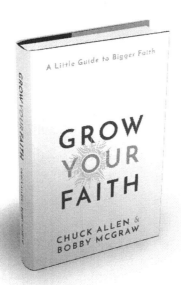

If "Grow Your Faith: A Little Guide to Bigger Faith" has sparked something in you, we'd love for you to visit GrowYourFaithBook.com. This companion website is here to help you take your spiritual journey even further.

At GrowYourFaithBook.com, you can:

- Connect with Chuck Allen and Bobby McGraw, the authors behind the book.

- Access exclusive content designed to help you grow.

- Get a behind-the-scenes look at the making of the book and the stories that inspired it.

Plus, you'll be the first to know about upcoming events, new releases, and special offers.

Don't miss out on this chance to dive deeper into the message of "Grow Your Faith." Head over to **GrowYourFaithBook.com** today and start exploring all the ways you can strengthen your faith journey!

T H E   W E E K D A Y
PODCAST

Encouragement to start each day. The first few minutes of each day are some of the most important minutes of the day. Join us every Monday – Friday as we spend time applying God's word to our lives. It's just 5 minutes a day, 5 days a week.

www.weekdaypodcast.com

In a world full of anger, anxiety, and negativity, we could all use a positive word. Each week, co-hosts, Chuck and Julie unpack the integration of faith and psychology. With encouragement and truth, you can discover your best you.

www.positivetalkpodcast.com

SUGARHILL
C H U R C H

Chuck and Bobby serve together at Sugar Hill Church in Northeast Georgia, and we'd love to connect with you— whether in person or online. At Sugar Hill Church, our mission is to help you know God and discover your purpose in Him. We're passionate about making a meaningful difference in our community and beyond.

Visit **www.sugarhill.church** to check out a recent message and plan your visit. We look forward to meeting you!

Made in the USA
Middletown, DE
03 September 2024

60239739R00113